T0340410

THE
World
IS YOUR
Dumpling

EMILY ROZ

THE World IS YOUR Dumpling

LITTLE PARCELS. BIG FLAVOURS.
80 GORGEOUS RECIPES.

PHOTOGRAPHY BY
HAARALA HAMILTON

HarperCollins*Publishers*

CONTENTS

RECIPES

INTRO

Hey hey hey, I'm Em! I'm guessing you're reading this because you absolutely love dumplings. Well, you're in luck, because this cookbook is full of dumpling recipes inspired by here, there and everywhere. I could start this introduction by talking all about me, but I'd much rather talk about this wonderful food group: the dumpling. So let's get into it.

WHAT IS A DUMPLING?

I could attempt to give you a very 'dictionary-style' definition but I just don't think that's possible when it comes to defining a dumpling. I'll get on to their physical features in a second, but for me a dumpling is something that brings with it a certain amount of nostalgia; dumplings make people smile, and they're the epitome of comfort. Regardless of culture, country or religion, most cuisines of the world have something that they call a dumpling, and I think that's a beautiful thing. Whether they're stuffed or rolled, steamed or boiled, made as an everyday meal, or as a celebratory dish for a special occasion, they're a universal language for good, happy food.

You might have noticed dumplings soaring in popularity in recent years, but they've been living with us for centuries. In homes across the world, the art of making dumplings is a ritual, a meditation – often a multi-generational family affair. Ancestors from times long gone have passed down secret recipes for future generations to savour and enjoy. They are dishes that we've relished as children, and recipes that we get to make for our loved ones as time goes on ... maybe that's why we think of them with such fondness.

For those unfortunate enough not to be brought up around dumplings, they can appear intimidating to make from scratch – I understand the hesitancy. With a bombardment of perfectly plump, carefully crimped and fabulously formed dumplings omnipresent on social media and in restaurants, we naturally question our ability to replicate these perfect little parcels. Yet, homemade

dumplings are honestly some of the simplest food items that will ever grace your kitchen table. I'm a firm believer that no dumpling is ugly; at the end of the day, if you've followed my simple recipes, used the correct ingredients and remembered to add in a dollop of love, they'll always taste delicious. So dust off your apron, whip out your rolling pin and let's get stuck in.

Sorry, hold on a second, I might have gotten a tad carried away there ... (put the rolling pin back people). We've encountered the emotional and nostalgic side of dumplings, but we haven't really talked about what a dumpling actually is. And that's because it's hard. A dumpling can mean sooo many different things, to sooo many different people. The footprint of this 'food group' (yes, I'm going there) reaches so far and wide, you would be remiss to think they weren't going for global culinary domination. These cheeky little munchkins can be soft and fluffy, filled-to-bursting, sweet and savoury, and come in all shapes and sizes. Italian ravioli (see page 173), Polish pierogi (see page 111) or Turkish manti (see page 61) are the European versions of Chinese jiaozi (see page 94) or Uzbek chuchvara (see page 100) – essentially we are talking about some sort of dough wrapper encasing a meat or veggie filling, that is then boiled, steamed or fried. You've then got fluffy dumplings like British suet dumplings (see page 90) or Botswanaian madombi (see page 144) – here dough balls are typically placed on top of some kind of stew and steamed until fluffy. Hungarian túrógombóc (see page 189), German spaetzle (see page 129) or Dominican domplines (see page 69) are small boiled dumplings, generally without a filling, also known as 'naked dumplings'. Now, when it comes to baked dumplings, there's a bit of a blurred line between pie, pastry and dumpling. To be as inclusive as possible (but mainly because they taste so good), I've chosen to embrace what I see as the dumpling's first cousins; some of my favourites include Argentine empanadas (see page 108), Greek spanakopita (see page 120) and North American baked apples (page 188). There are literally hundreds of dumplings out there and to make things even more interesting I've included dishes that are inspired by some even more distant dumpling family members, like my Uzbek oromo (see page 114), Portuguese rissois de carne (see page 150), Chinese cabbage rolls (see page 135) and Jamaican fried dumplings (see page 130).

I hope that gives you a better idea about what a dumpling is, or just how generic the term can be! Check out the illustration on pages 30–31, which brings the dumpling's journey across the world to life.

A BIT ABOUT ME

Firstly, I want to say a big thank you for being here. It really means the world to me, especially because this is my first cookbook (aaaah!). So, you're probably thinking, why a dumpling book and why you?! The short answer is because I love dumplings. The long answer is as follows:

I grew up all over Europe. Starting in Poland, followed by the Czech Republic, then France, England, Switzerland and then back to England (what a palaver ... absolutely loved it). Having a childhood abroad left me with not only an awareness and love for international foods, but immersed me in the welcoming, authentic and vibrant kitchens of friends and families from all over the world. Being exposed to different cultures and cuisines fuelled my desire to explore the world of food as I got older. My partner Henry and I have been lucky enough to travel across South America, China and large chunks of Europe, plucking morsels of local delicacies from the market stalls of sleepy villages, charming provincial towns and bustling metropolises. I have always loved the classic British dumplings (my mum would make a cracking beef stew with suet dumplings), but it was during our travels and time abroad that my love for *other* dumplings grew immensely. I learned how to make Chinese jiaozi while staying in a homestay at the base of the Great Wall in Gubeikou, ate bucket-loads of ravioli, agnolotti and casoncelli while travelling to Rome and Northern parts of Italy, and gazed at the production line of Chilean empanadas in small huts on the sides of barren plains while road-tripping in the Andes.

After returning from China in my final year of university, I made jiaozi and wonton-inspired dumplings on the reg. I would use the dumpling-making process as a stress-reliever, and the result was a moment of happiness* (*distraction from work). My friends and I would host 'dumpling nights', where we would sit together to make them from scratch before proceeding to devour our creations while giggling, chatting and truly enjoying life (with a large glass or two of vino ... obviously).

After university, I got a job in marketing but worked as a part-time breakfast chef to hone my culinary skills on the side. It was around this time that I decided I really wanted to work in the food industry as a recipe developer, so I set up Myriad Recipes as an online portfolio in an attempt to appeal to my would-be future employers. During this process I started a series called 'Around the world in 80 dumplings', where I researched, explored and shared my take on 80 different dumplings from around the globe. It was unbelievably eye-opening and honestly took my passion for cooking (and dumplings) to new heights. I never intended to gain a following from my social media accounts, so it was a big surprise when people began engaging, following and loving the series. So much so that my online community grew to over 200,000 within the first few months (whaaaat?!).

I left my marketing and breakfast chef jobs to pursue a career in recipe development. I wanted to keep improving my cooking knowledge though, so I began working as a chef at Noya's Kitchen, a Vietnamese restaurant in Bath. Working with Noya and the team was an absolute joy. Every shift was filled with laughter, learnings and lots of good food. I absolutely loved working as a chef there, but as time went on, the positive response from my audience led me to focus entirely on Myriad Recipes. I now live in London (big smoke time), where I'm surrounded by a melting pot of cultures, food and people. I'm able to do what I love every single day because of the support from people like you!

A bit of soppiness: if you'd told me in 2021 that I'd be writing a cookbook, I would have thought you were having a laugh. It's been a dream of mine to write a cookbook as food is a massive part of my life. Getting creative in the kitchen and then seeing the smiles on peoples' faces when they devour something I've made is honestly THE best feeling. So, thank you. And I hope this book brings you as much joy as it did to me while making it.

Sending hugs and dumplings,

Em x

HOW TO

USE THIS BOOK

If I can give you one piece of advice on how to use this book, it would be to read the recipe from start to finish before attempting to make it. Don't worry, there are no nasty surprises in this book (I'm talking about those frustrating recipes that say they'll take 30 minutes but then it says you need to leave it to chill for 3 hours), but it's always wise to know what you're getting into. You'll have a better idea of what happens, when it happens and what ingredients and tools you'll need. Trust me, it'll make your life much easier, and on a jolly note, get you buzzed about making the recipe!

THE LAYOUT

I've decided to structure the book to ease you into making dumplings, chapter by chapter, with some 'cheat' recipes right at the end for when you've had a long day but still want that dumpling fix. We begin with Easy Breezy Meals, where we'll be making dumplings from scratch, mostly using store-bought wrappers, although you always have the option to make your own wrappers if you have more time. Making these recipes is a breeze, and lots of fun. The next chapter is where we move up a level on the dumpling-making scale. These are the 30 minute+ recipes, also known as A Bit More Effort, Maximum Satisfaction, which tells you that they will require a little bit more time and effort to make. But seriously, don't be nervous, it's only a bit of dough, and a few other ingredients and they are all delicious and are absolute crowd-pleasers so I hope you feel they are worth it. Speedy Eats is where you'll find the recipes that'll take you just over 10 minutes to make. These are all quick and very simple recipes if you've got a dumpling craving but have little to no energy. It's all about playing with flavour and making something super tasty with dumplings. So whether you make these recipes with homemade dumplings or store-bought ones, I won't judge, I just want you to have fun. Last but not least, the final chapter is where you'll find Sweet Treats. Although I don't have a huge sweet tooth myself, I can tell you that these will get anyone going.

A FEW WORDS ON FOOD CULTURE

This book is all about appreciating food and the cultures and countries it comes from. As someone who has grown up in several countries and adores travelling to different parts of the world, I have a passion for ingredients, techniques and stories from here, there and everywhere. I have made a very conscious decision to not give any of the recipes in this book their 'authentic' names, because I'll be the first to admit that my recipes aren't authentic, and they were never intended to be. The intention was always to bring light to dishes, ingredients and ways of cooking from countries that have inspired me to cook, share and eat with the people I love. They're a celebration of dumplings and flavours from around the world that have been brought together harmoniously to make a symphony of mouthwatering dishes.

For that reason each recipe includes a brief description about its origins and my inspiration for making it. Every recipe is a celebration of the humble dumpling, and an attempt to highlight this diverse food group. They come in all shapes and sizes, forms, textures and tastes. They're beautiful things and nearly every country in the world has one to call their own. Whether it's jiaozi from China, suet dumplings from the UK, empanadas from Argentina or pierogi from Poland, dumplings are everywhere and can be enjoyed by everyone.

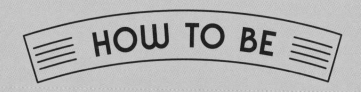

HOW TO BE

A QUICK (AND SUCCESSFUL!) DUMPLING COOK

One of the misconceptions about dumpling making is that it takes a long time. So, here are a few tips and tricks that will help you make dumplings in a speedy and efficient way, and will guarantee to shorten the time that you spend in the kitchen.

1

DON'T JUDGE A BOOK BY ITS COVER
If you're just beginning your dumpling-making journey, don't fret too much about how they look. Treat each attempt as a chance to improve, because even if they're not picture-perfect, they'll still taste fantastic.

2

ORGANISE, PREP AND MEASURE OUT YOUR INGREDIENTS
This may seem like a very obvious tip, but honestly, picking out the ingredients,

measuring them and prepping beforehand makes everything way more efficient. I like to get out all my spices/sauces and bundle them to one side of the worktop, then get some little bowls and use them to measure out any dough, water or bulkier ingredients. Trust me, it'll make your life easier!

3

TIME-MANAGEMENT AND MULTI-TASKING
As I mentioned previously, one of the reasons that I recommend reading the recipe all the way through before cooking, is because you can pre-plan what you're going to do and when. All of my recipes are structured and written in a way to promote using your time in the most efficient way, but nonetheless, you might find something that works better for you, so crack on and you do you honey!

4

FOUR HANDS ARE BETTER THAN TWO

All of these recipes can be easily made by one person, however, if you enjoy cooking with other people, then it'll obviously speed up the process if you work together. They can chop while you fry, you can both assemble the dumplings together, double-timing the speed, and then you can both clean while the finishing touches of magic happen in the background.

5

SEASON, SEASON, SEASON

One of the best tips and tricks I can give you is to season your dumplings and any accompanying bits. It's one of the reasons why restaurant food can taste much better than home cooked food, because the amount of seasoning (salt, pepper, sugar, spice) added is a lot more than you'd traditionally use at home. For any dumpling with a filling, it's essential to season it well. If it tastes bland before you stuff it into your wrapper, trust me, it will be even more tasteless as a dumpling. To test it, cook a spoonful of the filling by frying it, and taste to see what the flavour is like. You want it to be a level or two higher than you'd like it to be, in terms of strength in flavour, because the wrapper will mute the flavour slightly once cooked.

6

LEFTOVERS FOR A RAINY DAY

There's nothing better than getting to the end of the day and racking your brains for what to make for dinner, only to realise that you've got a bunch of leftover dumplings in the freezer. So, if I'm not pushed for time, I'll always make more than the recipe asks, just so I can store them away in the fridge or freezer for a rainy day.

7

DUMPLINGS HAVE NO RULES

I love to experiment with dumplings and I urge you to do so too. With all of my recipes, I've provided detailed instructions and ingredient measurements. But if you don't like a certain vegetable, meat or method, switch it up and give your way a go!

8

LESS IS MORE

There are two parts to this tip. Part 1: when you're making a filled dumpling, you want to seriously avoid overfilling it, as it can make the folding process rather cumbersome. Start by adding 1–2 teaspoons of filling into the centre of the dumpling and wrapping up around it to give you more control of the shaping and pleating. As you become more confident, you can add in more filling, bit by bit. Part 2 is for the 'naked dumplings'. Most of these expand when cooked, so be mindful not to make the initial dumpling balls too big. Throughout the book, I've provided diameter measurements of how big I'd recommend them to be (pre-cooking).

9

STORE-BOUGHT OR HOMEMADE

For ease and speed, store-bought dumpling wrappers are a fabulous option. I have packets of round and square dumpling wrappers in my freezer that I defrost when I'm craving some pockets of joy. I also often buy fresh wrappers so I can use them straight away. That being said, making your own wrappers is very simple, and most recipes consist of just flour and water, making them incredibly pantry-friendly.

10

JUST ENJOY IT!

Making dumplings is far from a stressful endeavour. Like cooking in general, it's a fun activity that can be a great place to relax, spend time with friends and then gobble up the result. So use this book to get experimental and have a great time doing it.

INGREDIENTS

～ EVERY DUMPLING LOVER NEEDS ～

There's nothing worse than buying an ingredient for a recipe that you then never ever use again. I've tried to provide recipes throughout this cookbook that are diverse in flavour, but won't leave you with a dozen random pots of herbs and spices that get lost at the back of your cupboard. So, here are my pantry staples that I always have as a daily dumpling maker.

☐ **FLOUR:**
plain (all-purpose) flour, self-raising (self-rising) flour, glutinous rice flour, cornflour (cornstarch)

☐ **RAISING AGENTS:**
baking powder and instant yeast

☐ **SPICES:**
paprika, cumin, garam masala, turmeric, cinnamon

☐ **OILS:**
olive oil, sesame oil, vegetable oil (for frying)

☐ **WRAPPERS:**
rice paper, wonton, round, square

☐ **SALT AND PEPPER:**
good flaky salt and black pepper that you freshly grind

☐ **HERBS:**
dried oregano and thyme and fresh parsley, mint and coriander (cilantro)

☐ **NUTS AND SEEDS:**
sesame, sunflower, cashews, peanuts, walnuts

☐ **BEANS:**
chickpeas (garbanzo beans), lentils, butter beans, cannellini beans

☐ **SAUCES:**
light and dark soy sauce, hoisin sauce, chilli oil, fish sauce, hot sauce

☐ **VINEGARS:**
balsamic vinegar, rice wine vinegar

☐ **PASTES:**
gochujang, rose harissa, miso, tahini, 'nduja, chipotle, Thai red curry paste

☐ **STOCK CUBES:**
vegetable, fish, chicken and beef

☐ **NOODLES:**
wide rice noodles, egg noodles, soba noodles

TOOLS

I'm not going to lie, I don't have bags of kitchen space, so only owning equipment that is everyday essential is how I roll. Plus, dumplings are technology minimalists, meaning they're actually very low maintenance. While a food processor and rolling pin are valuable tools to invest in, you definitely don't need either of them to have a great time with this book (a good knife to finely chop the ingredients and a bottle of wine to roll out the dough should suffice). This book is all about minimal effort and maximum satisfaction, so the fewer pieces of equipment needed, the better I say. So, here are a few bits and bobs I have lying around my kitchen at all times:

MIXING BOWL
If you don't have one of these, I urge you to get one ... a large one. Any one will do, whether it's stainless steel, glass, ceramic or silicone. We'll be using it to mix all of our dough and fillings.

CLING FILM (PLASTIC WRAP)
I am very aware that this is a single-use plastic, but please don't hate me, because it is a very handy way of wrapping dough, and I haven't found anything that does the job as well. However, if you're a firm no single-use plastic user, then you could try using beeswax wraps, but there's a risk they will stick to the dough, which makes it a bit of a faff. The same goes for foil. Your best bet would be to get some silicone wraps that you cover over your bowl, to leave your dough to rest.

ROLLING PIN
A large wooden rolling pin and a small wooden (no handles) rolling pin are two of my favourite tools to use. You want the large one to do all your big dough rolling (which you then cut into wrappers using cookie cutters), and although you don't actually *need* it, a smaller one to roll out individual small circular wrappers will make your life easier.

GOOD KNIVES
I know this sounds obvious but trust me when I say that they make a big difference, and speed up the process enormously. I use an 18–20cm (7–8in) chef's knife for virtually all my chopping. I also use a paring knife (mini chef's knife) to do more of the fiddly bits. Make sure to regularly sharpen them (every 2 months or so).

CHOPPING BOARD

I use a really big wooden chopping board, not only for chopping, but for lining up my dumplings, ready to be cooked. But any board will suffice, as long as you've got a bit of clean work surface too.

FOOD PROCESSOR

I use this a lot to speed up the chopping process when I have a handful of ingredients that need to be made into a rough paste.

BLENDER

Any blender will do, including a hand-held or stick blender – as long as you've got a jug to blend everything in! A blender is great for whizzing up many of the sauces in this book.

COOKIE CUTTERS

I sometimes just use a glass to cut out dumpling wrappers so you can too but cookie cutters will make life slightly easier.

CASSEROLE DISH

I love a good casserole dish, because they're multi-purpose. You can make a big old stew on the hob, whack in the dumplings and then bake in the oven until ready.

STEAMER

I'd recommend investing in a bamboo steamer, or you can use a stainless-steel steamer. If you can buy one with multiple layers, that would be even better!

NON-STICK FRYING PAN (SKILLET)

This is rather important, because quite a few of the recipes in the book require a very non-stick pan. Make sure that the pan also has a lid!

SAUCEPANS

A small saucepan and a large one would be grand.

GRATER

A box grater is what I use; it's got all the features and is easily accessible.

MICROWAVE

This will make your life a lot easier, trust me.

AIR FRYER

If you haven't already jumped on to the air fryer trend, let me be another person to tell you to. Honestly, it's a game changer. Let me put it this way, what would take you 40 minutes in the oven (includes preheating), takes 10 in the air fryer.

PASTA MACHINE

Right, I'll be honest … you do not *need* this. But, it's quite challenging to get pasta dough super-duper thin with just a rolling pin, so a pasta machine really does come in handy. Don't let not having one of these stop you from making pasta dough though. I've made it loads of times without – it just requires a bit more muscle power.

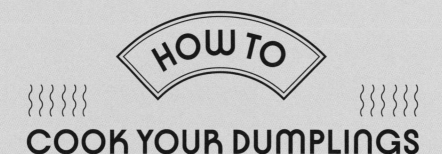

COOK YOUR DUMPLINGS

The most important thing to remember when it comes to dumplings, is NOT to overcook them! Overcooking leads to dry fillings and an unhappy consumer. Dumplings cook WAY faster than you think; I am constantly reassuring people in my Instagram comments who ask me whether 7 minutes is enough time to cook them ... and the answer is always yes. I've tried and tested these recipes dozens of times, and I promise you the timings I've given you are correct. So please don't overcook them. There are a few different methods when it comes to cooking dumplings and which one you choose will often depend on the type of dumpling you are cooking.

STEAMING

To steam your dumplings, you want a flat-based steamer so that you can fit as many dumplings on it as possible. I typically use a metal steamer that sits above one of my sauté pans but bamboo steamers aren't very expensive, so you could go for them too! Find one that fits on top of your saucepan or frying pan (skillet). I recommend steaming most dumplings over a medium heat but I'll be specific in the recipes as to what intensity of steaming they'll need.

PAN-FRYING

This is one of my favourite ways to cook dumplings as it gives you a juicy, soft dumpling with a crispy bottom – delicious. You'll need a non-stick frying pan (skillet) with a suitable lid. Place the pan over a medium heat, drizzle in a bit of oil and fry the dumplings so the bottoms get slightly crispy, then add some water and cover the pan with a lid so they 'pan-steam'. The lid is removed for the final couple of minutes to let any leftover water evaporate and for the bottoms of the dumplings to get super crispy.

BOILING

This is arguably the easiest way to cook dumplings, for which you'll need a saucepan with or without a lid. Bring salted water to the boil, then lower the heat to a simmer and gently drop the dumplings into the water (if the water is boiling too vigorously the dumplings can burst open). Once cooked, remove with a slotted spoon.

DEEP-FRYING

I must admit, I'm not a huge fan of deep-frying. However, there are a couple of delicious recipes that require it. I tend to use sunflower or vegetable oil for deep-frying and a large, heavy-based saucepan. Pour in the necessary amount of oil (but make sure it doesn't come more than halfway up the sides of the pan) and place over a medium heat. To check if the oil is ready, get a chopstick or a wooden spoon and place it into the oil, getting the end of the chopstick or wooden spoon to touch the base of the pan. If bubbles start to form and fizz around the chopstick or spoon, the oil is ready.

AIR FRYING

Air fryers are a great alternative to deep-frying if you want a crisp dumpling and if you have one of these you are probably already a fan of air frying. Air fryers do vary though so I've tried to be as clear as possible in my instructions when using air fryers. You'll want to keep an eye on them while they're cooking.

BAKING

Several recipes require an oven, so if you know your oven has certain tendencies to be overly hot or underperform, then go with your gut on temperatures, based on the ones I've suggested.

DUMPLING TYPES

PIEROGI
POLAND

SUET
UNITED KINGDON

BAKED APPLE DUMPLING
NORTH AMERICA

HALLACA
VENEZUELA

EMPANADA
ARGENTINA

MADOMBI
BOTSWANA

SOUSKLUITJIES
SOUTH AFRICA

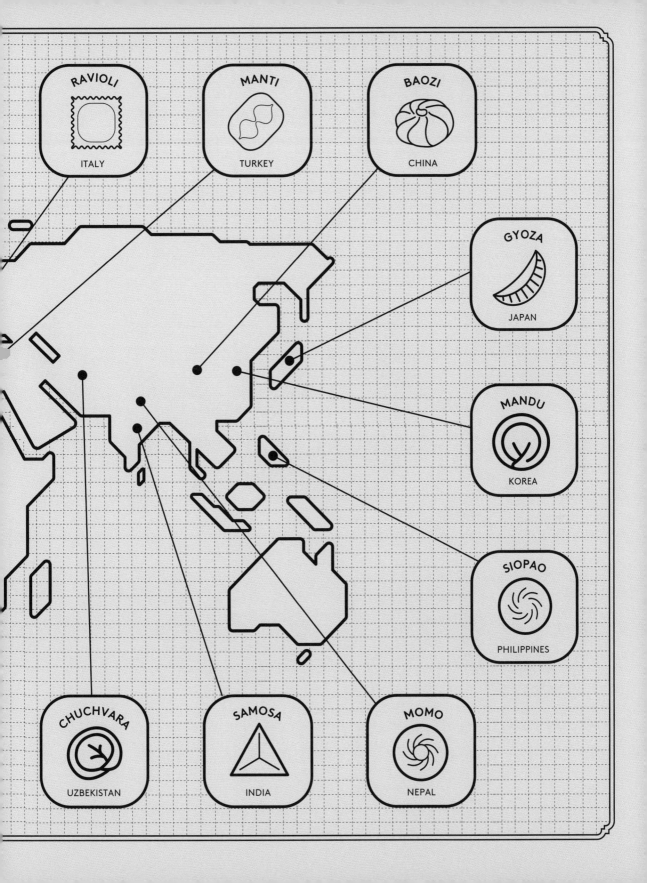

10 WAYS TO FOLD OR PLEAT A DUMPLING

SQUARE KITE

PLEATED STOOD-UP
SEMICIRCLE

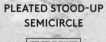

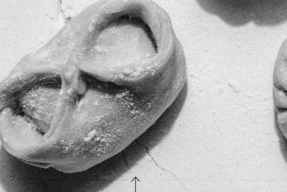

SPIRALLED
CIRCLE

BINOCULARS

WAVY

PLEATED
LIE-DOWN
SEMICIRCLE

LITTLE HAT

EASY
SEMICIRCLE

EASY PLEATED
STOOD-UP
SEMICIRCLE

SIMPLE
TRIANGLE

DIET

SYMBOLS

I'm very fortunate (I hope I'm not jinxing this) that I don't currently have any dietary requirements or intolerances. However, it's very common to have dietary requirements, and there's nothing worse than reading a recipe, loving the sound of it and then realising you can't eat it. Furthermore, if you're cooking for a friend who has a dietary requirement, it's important to understand the ingredients you can and can't use. So to help you out, I've provided a key for each recipe, which will tell you whether it's vegan, vegetarian, non-vegetarian (contains meat or fish) or is gluten- or dairy-free. However, it's now increasingly easy to make swaps based on your dietary requirements so at the back of the book you'll find a helpful section that tells you all the different ways you can adapt the recipes, whether that's using gluten-free wrappers, plant-based milk or cheese or swapping the meat filling for a veggie one. Here's what the little symbols mean:

VEGAN

This refers to recipes whereby all animal products and by-products are excluded, meaning no meat, poultry, fish, dairy, eggs, honey or any other animal-derived ingredients. Make sure to check that all the ingredients (especially sauces that you use) are vegan.

VEGGIE

One step along from vegan, this refers to a recipe that excludes meat and seafood. However, vegetarians can still eat by-products of animals like eggs, dairy and honey so the recipes may include them.

NON-VEGGIE

This symbol implies that the dish includes some form of meat or fish. If you're looking to add some animal protein to a meal, you'll also see on pages 201–212 that I've provided some simple suggestions in many of the vegan and veggie recipes in this book.

DAIRY-FREE

This indicates that a recipe contains zero dairy products i.e. it excludes all products derived from milk or milk-producing animals. This includes cow's milk, goat's milk and sheep's milk, as well as products made from these milks, such as cheese, yoghurt, butter, cream and ice cream.

GLUTEN-FREE

This refers to a recipe that excludes gluten – a protein found in wheat, barley, rye and their derivatives. For individuals with coeliac disease, gluten sensitivity or wheat allergy, consuming gluten can cause adverse reactions ranging from stomach problems such as gastrointestinal discomfort to serious health complications. So, if someone tells you that they're gluten free, please take it seriously! Those following a gluten-free diet strictly avoid foods containing gluten to manage their condition and maintain optimal health.

STAPLE RECIPES

Before we go on to the main recipes, I thought I'd provide a few basics to get you started: three dough wrapper recipes and two filling recipes.

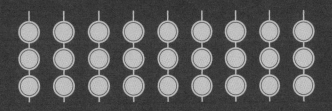

Water & Flour Wrappers

200g (7oz) plain (all-purpose) flour,
plus extra for dusting
¼ tsp salt

1. Pour the flour and salt into a large bowl.
2. Gently pour in 100ml (3½fl oz) water and mix with your hands or chopsticks until a shaggy dough forms. Knead for 30 seconds until a rough dough forms. Cover in cling film (plastic wrap) and set aside while you make your filling.
3. After your dough has rested, knead for another minute until the dough is smooth and bouncy.
4. Poke a hole through the centre of the dough and then continue to stretch it to form a thin-ringed doughnut (with a large hole). Slice the doughnut and form it into a long log around 4cm (1½in) in diameter. Cut 16–20 pieces from the dough.
5. Keep the wrappers under a towel or cling film, and one by one, roll out each wrapper into a 10cm (4in) circle around 2–3mm (⅛in) thick. Then, continue on with your dumpling recipe!

HOW TO STORE

1. Fridge: Brush your wrappers with starch (potato or tapioca) using a small brush or your fingers, so it covers the entire surface of the wrapper. This prevents them from sticking together. Do not use plain (all-purpose) flour as this just absorbs into the wrappers, making them stick together. Stack the wrappers, brushing with starch as you go, then wrap the stack in cling film, place in an airtight container and into the fridge. Use within 1–2 days.

2. Freezer: Follow the instructions above using starch to brush over the entire surface of the wrapper, stack, then place them in the freezer for up to 3 months. Let the wrappers defrost on your work surface until soft, about 3–4 hours.

Egg & Flour Wrappers

200g (7oz) '00' flour, plus extra
for dusting
2 large eggs

1. Tip the flour out on to a clean work surface or large chopping board and form it into a mound, making a well in the centre.
2. Crack the eggs into the centre of the well and gently break the yolks pulling the flour in from around the well into the centre using a fork. Incorporate the flour in with the eggs until a shaggy dough starts to form. If the dough is too dry, add a splash of water to loosen.
3. Once a rough dough forms, use your hands and start kneading until you get a smooth yellow dough (you'll want to knead for a good few minutes).
4. Wrap the dough in cling film (plastic wrap) and place in the fridge to rest while you make your filling of choice.
5. When you're ready to make your dumplings, remove the dough from the fridge and knead for another 30 seconds, then cut in half and set one aside, covering with a towel or wrapping in cling film to prevent it from drying out.
6. If you've got a pasta machine, fantastic. If not, then a rolling pin will suffice!
7. Flour your machine or surface and roll one of the pieces of dough out until paper thin. If you're using a pasta machine, keep going down the size levels until you get to the thinnest setting. Dust over some flour to prevent the pieces sticking together.
8. Repeat this process with the other piece of dough, then continue with your dumpling recipe, fill and cook!

HOW TO STORE

1. Fridge: If you want to store the pasta dough ball as a whole in the fridge, sprinkle it with flour and then wrap it in cling film. Place it in a container or ziplock bag and keep in the fridge for 1–2 days.
2. Freezer: You can also freeze your pasta ball. Follow the instructions above and then freeze for up to 3 months. If you want to freeze the pasta in wrappers, dust them with starch, then place them on top of each other and wrap cling film around the stack. Place in a ziplock bag and freeze for up to 3 months. Defrost thoroughly for 2–3 hours at room temperature before using.

Gluten-free Wrappers

100g (3½oz) rice flour
50g (scant 2oz) glutinous rice flour
50g (scant 2oz) tapioca starch
½ tsp salt
Cornflour (cornstarch), if needed

1. In a large bowl, combine the rice flour, glutinous rice flour, tapioca starch and salt. Give it a whisk, then add 250ml (9fl oz) water and whisk until a smooth, lump-less batter-y dough forms.
2. Cover the bowl with cling film (plastic wrap) and place in the microwave for 2 minutes.
3. Remove from the microwave and mix using a spatula to try to combine the dough. Cover once again with cling film and place back into the microwave for a further 2 minutes.
4. Remove from the microwave. You should have a firm but bouncy dough. Give it a good knead with the spatula because it will be hot. Remove from the bowl and place onto a clean surface. Leave to cool until you can knead it by hand.
5. Once cool enough to handle, knead by hand, sprinkling over some cornflour if needed. It should be a firm, bouncy, non-sticky dough.
6. Form into a ball and then poke a hole through the middle, then continue to stretch it to form a doughnut (with a large hole). Slice into 16–20 equal pieces.
7. Take one piece at a time and roll using a rolling pin into circular wrappers around 8–10cm (20–25in) in diameter.

HOW TO STORE

1. Fridge: To store, brush each wrapper with cornstarch, lay on top of each other, and cover in clingfilm. Place in the fridge for up to 3 days.

2 Freezer: Sprinkle the dough ball with starch and then wrap in cling film and place in a ziplock bag. Freeze for up to 3 months. Defrost thoroughly for 3 hours at room temperature before using.

Meat-based Filling

200g (7oz) high-fat (10–20%)
  minced meat (turkey, beef,
  chicken, pork)
1 small white onion, finely chopped
2 garlic cloves, finely chopped or
  grated
1 tsp flaky salt
1 tsp ground black pepper

1. Combine all the ingredients in a bowl and mix until smooth. Add any seasonings based on the recipe or experiment with your own flavour combinations (see the flavour table opposite).

Veg-based Filling

100g (3½oz) firm tofu, crumbled
50g (scant 2oz) cabbage,
  roughly chopped
50g (scant 2oz) mushrooms,
  roughly chopped
1 small white onion, roughly
  chopped
2 garlic cloves, finely chopped
  or grated
2 tsp flaky salt
1 tsp ground black pepper
Equipment: straining cloth

1. Place all the ingredients into a food processor and blend until a finely chopped mixture has formed.
2. Remove from the blender and transfer to a sieve lined with a straining cloth. Bring all the sides of the cloth up and then, over the sink, twist the cloth so that the filling gets squeezed at the base. Keep twisting to squeeze any excess water or liquid out of the cloth. Once no more liquid is coming out, your filling is ready to go. Season it with the ingredients in your chosen recipe, or experiment with your own flavours (see the flavour table opposite).

THE FLAVOUR TABLE

What I'd love for you to take from this book is a fondness for experimentation. Food can be fun, creative and random, which is why I've provided a flavour table for you to have a play with. These are the herbs, seasonings, pastes and sauces that I use on a regular basis, followed by a handful of fun flavour profiles for you to try out.

Quick tip: When it comes to quantities, I tend to follow a basic rule of thumb – for dried herbs I add by the teaspoon, while for fresh herbs I tend to add around 10g (scant ½oz) of chopped herbs as this adds a good amount of flavour but isn't overpowering. For seasonings, once again, I add by the teaspoon. But then when it comes to pastes and sauces, I'll add by the tablespoon because I want to really taste that desired flavour.

Here are a few flavour profiles I've put together – I love these combinations but feel free to mix and match your own! The following examples are based on using 200g (7oz) of a main filling ingredient such as meat mince or a plant-based alternative.

THE BUFFALO – 2 tbsp buffalo sauce, 20g (generous ½oz) chives, 1 tsp paprika.

THE FRESH ONE – 10g (scant ½oz) fresh coriander (cilantro), 10g (scant ½oz) fresh mint, 1 fresh chilli, 1 tbsp rice wine vinegar, 1 tbsp sugar.

THE HARISSA – 10g (scant ½oz) fresh parsley, 1 tsp paprika, 1 tsp cumin, 1 tbsp rose harissa.

THE GUCCHI-JANG – 10g (scant ½oz) chives, 1 tsp gochugaru flakes, 1 tbsp gochujang, 2 tbsp light soy sauce, 1 tbsp sesame oil, 1 tbsp rice wine vinegar, 1 tbsp sugar.

THE CHIPOTLE – 10g (scant ½oz) fresh coriander (cilantro), 1 tsp chilli flakes, 1 tsp sugar, 1 tbsp chipotle.

THE MILD – 1 tsp oregano, 1 tsp thyme, 5g (scant ¼oz) parsley, 1 tsp paprika.

THE CUMIN – 10g (scant ½oz) fresh coriander (cilantro), 1 tsp paprika, 1 tsp cumin, 1 tsp chilli flakes.

HERBS	SEASONINGS	PASTES	SAUCES
Oregano	Paprika	Tahini	Soy sauce
Thyme	Cumin	Rose Harissa	Sesame oil
Coriander (Cilantro)	Chilli flakes	Chipotle	Oyster sauce
Parsley	Gochugaru flakes	Gochujang	Buffalo sauce
Mint	Sugar		Rice wine vinegar
Chives			
Chilli			

EASY

20+MINS

For many of these recipes you can use the dumpling wrappers you've just learned how to make in Staple Recipes, but to keep things simple and straightforward, using store-bought wrappers is always an option. So, whack on some tunes and get cooking.

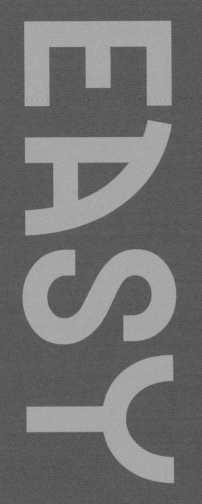

BREEZY

MEALS

Chilli Garlic Prawns with Ricotta Puffs

These ricotta puffs, or gnudi, are not a million miles away from gnocchi. Instead of being made with potato, they're traditionally assembled using ricotta cheese and semolina flour, giving them a light, pillowy feel compared to their denser, chewier cousin. To make this Italian-inspired recipe more accessible to the masses, I've used breadcrumbs instead of semolina flour. Chilli, garlic and prawns are a holy trio in my world, wonderfully coating the gnudi in all their bold flavours. You can adapt the size of the gnudi based on your preference. I like small, bite-sized portions about the size of a large grape, but you do you!

FOR THE GNUDI

250g (9oz) ricotta cheese
50g (scant 2oz) grated Parmesan cheese
1 small egg
6 tbsp breadcrumbs
¼ tsp grated nutmeg
plain (all-purpose) flour for dusting and rolling
Salt and pepper

FOR THE CHILLI GARLIC PRAWN SAUCE

2 tbsp olive oil
2 garlic cloves, minced
1–2 tsp chilli flakes
400g (14oz) raw prawns (shrimp)
400g (14oz) cherry tomatoes, finely chopped

TO GARNISH

Basil, roughly chopped
Grated Parmesan cheese

1. Place the ricotta cheese, grated Parmesan cheese, small egg, breadcrumbs, nutmeg and a pinch of salt and pepper in a large bowl. Mix with your hands or a wooden spoon gently.
2. Next, add the flour and mix. You are looking for a soft, slightly sticky texture but bounded enough to be able to roll into little balls. If it's too loose or sticky, add a tablespoon of flour at a time until you achieve the right consistency.
3. Once fully incorporated, gently wet your hands and roll the mixture into small neat balls around 15g (½oz) each in weight in the palm of your hands.
4. Pour some flour into a small bowl and toss the ricotta balls into the flour one by one, and set aside. Handle with care, they should be like light pillows.
5. To cook the gnudi, bring a large pan of salted water to a gentle simmer, and submerge the balls. Gently cook for 4 minutes or until they rise to the surface.
6. When your dumplings are nearly cooked, place a frying pan (skillet) over a medium heat and add in 2 tbsp olive oil.
7. Carefully remove the gnudi with a slotted spoon, drain off the excess water and add to your oiled pan. Fry on each side for 2 minutes until golden brown.
8. Next, add in your minced garlic, chilli flakes, raw prawns and chopped cherry tomatoes. Cook over a high heat for 4 minutes and toss frequently. Once the prawns are cooked and the tomatoes have softened, you're ready to eat.
9. Transfer your chilli garlic dumplings and prawns on to a serving platter and top with basil and Parmesan cheese.

Tofu & Broccoli Dumplings Glazed in Soy & Sesame Seed Dressing

This is my vegan take on the popular Japanese gyoza, although they actually originate from mainland China. Gyoza were introduced to Japan in the 1800s; their name comes from the way the Japanese pronounce the Chinese name jiaozi – aka potsticker dumplings for those in the West. These dumplings are super versatile, which is one of the reasons why they're so universally loved. I've chosen to fill them with a gorgeous tofu and broccoli mixture and glaze them in a soy sauce and sesame dressing. YUM!

FOR THE DUMPLINGS

100g (3½oz) firm tofu, crumbled
75g (2½oz) broccoli florets
2 garlic cloves
1cm (½in) piece of ginger, grated
3 tbsp light soy sauce
1 tbsp sesame oil
1 tbsp rice wine vinegar
1 tsp sugar
1 tsp ground black pepper
16–20 dumpling wrappers
   (ensure vegan and gluten-free)
1 tbsp vegetable oil

1. Begin by making the dumpling filling. Add the tofu, broccoli, garlic and ginger to a food processor or blender and blend to a rough paste. Transfer the mixture to a large bowl and add the light soy sauce, sesame oil, rice wine vinegar, sugar and black pepper. Mix thoroughly.

2. Next, get your dumpling wrappers. Working on one at a time (keep the rest under a damp tea towel so they don't dry out), lightly wet the edges of the wrapper with your finger and add a heaped teaspoon of the filling to the centre of the wrapper. Fold the wrapper in half over the filling and pinch at the top of the half circle with your fingers, but don't seal it yet.

3. Hold the wrapper in your left hand and starting near the top centre, fold a pleat on the top half of the wrapper using the thumb and index finger of your right hand – the pleat should turn towards the centre. (There are links to all dumpling folding methods on pages 32–33.) Use your left thumb and index finger to press the folded pleat tightly against the back half of the wrapper. Repeat the folding along the right side, making around 3–4 pleats. (For a quicker method, pinch and seal in the centre and then fold one pleat on each side of the dumpling, both facing inwards towards the centre – see image on page 33).

4. Continue with the left side of the dumpling, making 3–4 pleats with your left hand, starting in the centre and moving towards the left side with the pleats facing the centre. Press the pleats one last time to seal and shape the dumpling and create a flat side on the bottom. Repeat with the remaining wrappers and filling to complete all dumplings.

FOR THE DRESSING

3 tbsp light soy sauce

1 tbsp sesame oil

1 tsp cornflour (cornstarch) mixed
    with 3 tbsp water

1 tbsp rice wine vinegar

½ tbsp sugar

1 garlic clove, finely chopped
    or grated

1 tbsp chilli oil

TO GARNISH

2 spring onions (scallions),
    finely chopped

Sesame seeds

5. Place a large non-stick frying pan (skillet) over a medium heat and add the vegetable oil. Add the dumplings flat side down and fry for 2 minutes until slightly golden on the bottom. Pour in 50ml (1½fl oz) water, cover with a lid and cook for 4 minutes, or until the water evaporates.

6. Meanwhile, add all the dressing ingredients to a small saucepan and place over a medium heat. Cook for 2–3 minutes until the dressing has reduced and thickened. Turn off the heat and set it aside.

7. Remove the lid of your pan to evaporate any remaining water and to crisp up the bottom of the dumplings.

8. Transfer your dumplings to a serving plate and drizzle over the soy sesame glaze. Scatter over the chopped spring onions and sesame seeds and enjoy!

Miso Tofu Soup with Pork & Mushroom Pillows

SERVES 2-3
MAKES 16
DUMPLINGS

Umami, one of the five key taste profiles, is basically when something is really, really savoury. And this recipe is packed full of it. Miso is a fermented Japanese paste used in a wide variety of dishes and is no stranger to umami; it's slightly sweet, very salty, and when added in the perfect proportions, creates the ultimate savoury flavour bomb. This is my take on a classic Japanese miso soup, made with pork and mushroom dumplings, bobbing with silken tofu. It's really simple to make and one of my favourite soup recipes.

FOR THE DUMPLINGS

200g (7oz) mushrooms
1 small onion, roughly chopped
3 garlic cloves
2.5cm (1in) piece of ginger, roughly chopped
1 tbsp vegetable oil
200g (7oz) pork mince (ground pork)
1 tbsp white miso paste
½ tsp sugar
1 tsp ground black pepper
16 square egg and flour dumpling wrappers

FOR THE SOUP

1 litre (2 pints) vegetable stock
1½ tbsp miso paste
1 tsp light soy sauce
½ tbsp rice wine vinegar
250g (9oz) silken tofu, sliced into cubes

TO GARNISH

2 spring onions (scallions), finely chopped

1. Put the mushrooms, onion, garlic and ginger into a food processor and blitz until finely chopped; set aside.
2. Heat the oil in a frying pan (skillet) over a medium heat and add the pork. Fry for 2 minutes until browned all over, then add the mushroom mixture and fry for a further 5 minutes. Transfer to a large bowl, allow to cool, then add the miso paste, sugar and black pepper. Give everything a good mix and then get ready to assemble.
3. Put your square wrappers under a damp tea towel so they don't dry out while you assemble the dumplings. One by one, lightly wet the edges of each wrapper with your finger and add a heaped teaspoon of the filling to the centre of the wrapper. Fold the wrapper in half to make a triangle, then bring two of the triangle corners together, lightly brush the edges with water using your fingers and seal. Repeat with the remaining wrappers and filling.
4. Next up, add all the soup ingredients to a large saucepan and place over a medium heat. Give it a gentle mix and bring up to the boil, then reduce the heat to a simmer. Taste and adjust the seasoning.
5. Add the dumplings to the soup and let them simmer for 5 minutes. Divide the dumplings and soup between bowls, sprinkle with spring onions and enjoy!

Gochujang Sausage Pouches topped with Kimchi

SERVES 2-3

These are inspired by mandu, one of Korea's national dumplings. Now, I love gochujang – a slightly addictive Korean fermented red pepper paste – as much as the next person, but these sausage gochujang dumplings occupy a serious place in my go-to favourite recipes list. They're sweet and spicy, with joyous bites of kimchi dotted on top for that extra tang. Serve these to anyone and I guarantee you'll see a smile.

FOR THE DUMPLINGS

250g (9oz) good-quality pork
  sausages
1 red onion, finely chopped
2 garlic cloves, very finely chopped
2 tbsp gochujang
2 tbsp light soy sauce
1 tbsp sesame oil
1 tbsp rice wine vinegar
1 tbsp honey
16–20 round dumpling wrappers

FOR THE SAUCE AND TOPPINGS

1 tbsp honey
2 tbsp light soy sauce
2 tbsp water
2 tbsp rice wine vinegar
150g (generous 5oz) kimchi
2 spring onions (scallions),
  finely chopped
½ tbsp sesame seeds

1. Squeeze out the meat from the sausage casings into a bowl and add the chopped red onion, garlic, gochujang, light soy sauce, sesame oil, rice wine vinegar and honey. Mix gently to combine – don't overmix as you want it to stay light and airy.

2. Next, get your dumpling wrappers (make sure you keep them covered under a damp tea towel so they don't dry out). One by one, lightly wet the edges of the wrappers with your finger and add a heaped teaspoon of the filling to the centre of the wrapper. Fold the wrapper in half to make a semicircle and pinch to seal, then bring both ends of the semicircle towards the centre and pinch the ends together. Repeat for the rest of the dumplings.

3. Prepare a steamer by brushing it with a thin layer of oil (to prevent the dumplings sticking to the bottom) and placing it on top of a pan of simmering water. Place the dumplings inside, cover with the lid and steam for 8–10 minutes.

4. Meanwhile, combine the honey, light soy sauce, water and rice wine vinegar in a small bowl to make a dipping sauce.

5. Once your dumplings are cooked, serve them up on a plate and top each one with some kimchi, followed by a sprinkling of chopped spring onion and sesame seeds. Enjoy with your dipping sauce.

Fiery Leek Pockets with a Spiced Lentil Sauce

SERVES 2-3

Based on Afghan ashak (or aushak) – leek or chive dumplings topped with a tomato lentil sauce, garlic yoghurt and mint – this recipe is one to convert any legume avoiders as it's always a crowd-pleaser. It's comforting yet refreshing with the warmth of the fiery leeks and tang of the garlicky herbed yoghurt. Whip this up in less than half an hour and get ready to treat your taste buds.

FOR THE DUMPLINGS

2 tbsp olive oil
1 large leek (about 200g/7oz), rinsed and finely chopped
1 tsp flaky sea salt
1 tsp chilli powder
½ tsp ground black pepper
16–20 circular dumpling wrappers
Sliced mint or coriander (cilantro) leaves, to garnish
Lemon wedges, to garnish

FOR THE TOPPINGS

1 tbsp vegetable oil
1 onion, finely chopped
2 garlic cloves, very finely chopped
1 tsp paprika
2 tomatoes, finely chopped
2 tbsp tomato purée
200ml (7fl oz) vegetable stock
1 x 400g (14oz) tin lentils, drained and rinsed
Salt and pepper

FOR THE GARLIC YOGHURT

300g (10½oz) plain yoghurt
1 tsp dried mixed herbs
2 garlic cloves, very finely chopped
Chopped mint leaves, to garnish

1. Place a frying pan (skillet) over a medium heat and drizzle in 1 tablespoon of the olive oil. Add the leek, sea salt, chilli powder and ground black pepper and fry for 5 minutes until the leeks have softened, then transfer to a plate.

2. Meanwhile, heat the vegetable oil in a saucepan over a medium heat and add the onion, 2 garlic cloves, paprika and chopped tomatoes. Fry for 5 minutes, then add the tomato purée, vegetable stock, lentils, pepper and a generous pinch of flaky sea salt. Simmer over a low heat and stir occasionally for 10 minutes. The sauce is ready when it's reduced to a thick, ragu-style consistency. Taste and adjust the seasoning.

3. Next, get your dumpling wrappers (make sure you keep them covered under a damp tea towel so they don't dry out). One by one, lightly wet the edges of each dumpling wrapper with your finger and add a heaped teaspoon of the filling into the centre of the wrapper.

4. Fold over the wrapper into a semicircle and pinch to seal. Repeat this step to make all the dumplings.

5. Bring a large saucepan of salted water to the boil over a medium-low heat and add the remaining tablespoon of olive oil. Using a slotted spoon, gently lower in your dumplings and cook for 4–5 minutes over a low heat, or so that they're gently simmering, but not boiling.

6. Meanwhile, combine the yoghurt, dried mixed herbs and garlic in a bowl and top with chopped mint; set aside.

7. Scoop out the cooked dumplings and place them in a greased colander.

8. To serve, spread a couple of spoonfuls of the yoghurt sauce on each plate and top with the cooked dumplings. Spoon over the lentil sauce and a few more dollops of yoghurt sauce, then garnish with mint or coriander and lemon wedges.

SERVES 2-3

Pork & Water Chestnut 'Dumpling Tacos'

If you're thinking that this pork and chestnut 'dumpling taco' sounds like a modern social-media mash-up recipe, then you'd be correct. It's a mish mash of Chinese-style flavours with Mexican taco-style presentation. Arguably one of the easiest dumplings to fold, because, well, there is no folding ... just spreading. There are no compromises on flavour here, although I still haven't quite figured out the best way to eat them. Hands? Chopsticks? Knife and fork? I think you'll have to do what works best for you!

FOR THE DUMPLINGS

200g (7oz) pork mince (ground pork)

1cm (½in) piece of ginger, very finely chopped

3 garlic cloves, finely chopped

100g (3½oz) water chestnuts, finely chopped

2 spring onions (scallions), finely chopped

1 tsp sugar

2 tbsp light soy sauce

1 tbsp sesame oil

1 tbsp rice wine vinegar

1 tbsp fish sauce

16–20 round dumpling wrappers

Sunflower oil, for frying

FOR THE DIPPING SAUCE

3 tbsp light soy sauce

1 tbsp sugar

1 tbsp rice wine vinegar

1 tbsp chilli oil

1. Add all the dumpling ingredients (except the wrappers) to a large bowl and give everything a good mix until a paste forms.

2. Get your dumpling wrappers and place them under a damp tea towel or cloth to stop them from drying out.

3. One by one, take a wrapper and place 1 tablespoon of the filling on to the dumpling wrapper, spreading it right out to the edges of the wrapper and pressing down so that the filling sticks to the wrapper. Repeat for all the dumplings.

4. Place a non-stick frying pan (skillet) over a medium heat and drizzle with oil (if you can, get two frying pans on the heat to speed up the process as you can only fit about three dumpling tacos in the pan at one time). Place the dumpling tacos meat-side down into the pan and use the back of a spatula to 'smash' the dumplings down so they're totally flat. Fry for 4 minutes, then flip the dumplings over, pour in 1–2 tablespoons of water and cover with a lid. Cook for a further 2 minutes.

5. Repeat until all of your dumplings are cooked – keep the cooked dumplings warm on a plate covered in foil.

6. When you are ready to serve, combine all of your dipping sauce ingredients in a small bowl and serve alongside the cooked 'dumpling tacos'. Enjoy!

Crispy Rice Paper Rolls

SERVES 2-3

The first time I made these crispy rice paper dumplings, I ate them all in one go. For those of you who aren't familiar with the ingredient, rice paper is a type of wrapper made from rice flour, tapioca starch, salt and water. Most commonly, they're used in Vietnamese cuisine to make deliciously refreshing summer rolls (filled with vermicelli noodles, herbs, marinated meat and fresh veggies). This crispy version is filled with a more umami-centric mixture and then pan-fried. I love to eat them freshly cooked so they're warm and have a slight crunch.

FOR THE DUMPLINGS

150g (generous 5oz) firm tofu
100g (3½oz) cabbage, roughly chopped
1 small carrot, roughly chopped
1 spring onion (scallion), roughly chopped
2 tbsp vegetable oil
2 garlic cloves, finely chopped or grated
1cm (½in) piece of ginger, grated
3 tbsp light soy sauce
1 tbsp rice wine vinegar
1 tbsp sesame oil
1 tsp chilli flakes
1 tbsp sugar
12 rice paper sheets

FOR THE DIPPING SAUCE

2 tbsp gluten-free light soy sauce
1 tbsp water
1 tbsp sesame oil
1 tbsp rice wine vinegar
1 tbsp chilli oil
1 tsp honey or sugar
½ tbsp sesame seeds

1. Add the tofu, cabbage, carrot and spring onion to a food processor and blitz together until you have a chunky paste.
2. Heat 1 tablespoon of the vegetable oil in a large frying pan (skillet) over a medium heat, add the garlic and ginger and fry for a minute until aromatic. Add the tofu and vegetable mixture to the pan and give it a stir. Fry for a couple of minutes, then add the light soy sauce, rice wine vinegar, sesame oil, chilli flakes and sugar. Stir-fry for 3 minutes, then transfer the mixture to a plate and set aside to cool.
3. To assemble the dumplings, dip a rice paper sheet in a large bowl of warm water for a few seconds and then place on a clean cutting board. Place a heaped tablespoon of the filling into the centre of the rice paper sheet. The rice paper is ready to fold when it's just beginning to get sticky. If you're folding and nothing is sticking, just leave it for a few seconds and you'll see it begin to soften. Bring the bottom half of the sheet up and fold it over the filling, then fold in the left and right sides. Roll the dumpling away from you, sealing the fold. They should look like little tight square parcels. Set aside on a lightly oiled plate so that the rolls don't stick and repeat to use up the rest of the filling and rice paper sheets.
4. Place a large non-stick frying pan (skillet) over a medium heat and drizzle in the remaining tablespoon of vegetable oil.
5. Add the rice paper rolls (make sure they don't touch each other) and fry on each side for 2–4 minutes, or until golden and crispy. You may have to do this in two batches, or if you have two frying pans, that would be ideal!
6. Meanwhile, combine all the dipping sauce ingredients together in a small bowl.
7. Once the dumplings are ready, serve them up with the dipping sauce and enjoy immediately.

SERVES 2-3

Hoisin Chicken & Chive Crispy Skirt Dumplings

When travelling across China, I ate my body weight in jiaozi – arguably one of the best-known Chinese dumplings. I remember visiting the Great Wall in Gubeikou and watching our host rapidly assemble dozens of these dumplings. This version takes a more restaurant-style, modern approach, with a cornflour slurry forming that delightfully crispy bottom. They're bold in flavour, varied in texture and super juicy.

FOR THE DUMPLINGS

200g (7oz) chicken mince (ground chicken)

20g (generous ½oz) chives, finely chopped, plus a few to garnish

2 garlic cloves, finely chopped or grated

2.5cm (1in) piece of ginger, finely chopped or grated

2 tbsp hoisin sauce

1 tsp ground black pepper

16 round dumpling wrappers

2 tbsp vegetable oil

2 tsp cornflour (cornstarch) mixed with 4 tbsp water

FOR THE DIPPING SAUCE

2 tbsp light soy sauce

2 tbsp water

1 tbsp rice wine vinegar

1 tsp sugar

1 tbsp chilli oil

1. In a large bowl, combine the minced chicken, chives, garlic, ginger, hoisin sauce and black pepper until smooth and paste-like.

2. Next, get your dumpling wrappers out (make sure you keep them covered with a damp tea towel so they don't dry out). One at a time, lightly wet the edges of the dumpling wrappers with your finger and add a heaped teaspoon of the filling to the centre of the wrapper.

3. To seal the dumpling, fold the wrapper in half over the filling and use your fingers to pinch and seal the wrapper just at the top of the semicircle. Starting near the centre on one side, fold one pleat towards the centre, then repeat to make 2 more pleats. Repeat on the other side, forming 6 pleats in total. Pinch to seal. Repeat this step for all the dumplings.

4. Place a large non-stick pan (skillet)over a medium-high heat. It is crucial that you use a non-stick pan to ensure that the dumpling skirt releases from the pan easily. Add the vegetable oil to the pan and swirl it around, then arrange the dumplings in the pan, starting in the centre and spiralling outwards. Fry for 2 minutes.

5. Stir the cornflour mixture again and then pour it into the pan (be careful as the oil may splatter a bit). Make sure to pour it in evenly so that all the spaces between the dumplings are covered. Reduce the heat to low, cover the pan with a lid and cook for 5 minutes.

6. Meanwhile, combine all the dipping sauce ingredients together in a small bowl.

7. Remove the lid of the dumpling pan and cook for 2 minutes, or until the entire dumpling skirt looks golden and can break away from the bottom of the pan. Turn off the heat, then flip a large plate over and place it on top of the dumplings. Place one hand on the plate (take care not to burn yourself!) and the other hand on the handle of the pan and flip it over.

8. Serve immediately with your dipping sauce.

Teenie Tiny Parcels with Whipped Feta Yoghurt & Paprika Butter

Variations of manti can be found all over Turkey and in Central and Western Asian cuisines. My take on it is simple: full of complementary flavours and adorned with paprika butter and mint. The fiddly bit of this recipe comes in when you mention the size of the dumpling. There's a well-known saying in Turkey that the chef has done a good job if you can fit 40 manti dumplings on one spoon ... basically, the smaller, the better ... but also the more time-consuming. It's up to you to decide whether to keep the dumpling wrappers whole or to cut them into quarters for a more traditional dumpling. Both will be delicious.

FOR THE DUMPLINGS

150g (generous 5oz) 10% fat beef mince (ground beef)
1 small white onion, finely chopped
10g (scant ½oz) parsley, finely chopped
1 tsp flaky sea salt
1 tsp ground black pepper
1 tsp chilli powder
12–16 square dumpling wrappers, (8 x 8cm/3 x 3in), sliced into quarters

FOR THE FETA YOGHURT

200g (7oz) yoghurt
100g (3½oz) feta
2 garlic cloves, finely chopped or grated

FOR THE PAPRIKA BUTTER

2 tbsp butter
1 tbsp olive oil
2 tsp smoked paprika
1 tbsp finely chopped mint, to garnish

1. Combine all the filling ingredients, except the dumpling wrappers, together in a large bowl.
2. Lay your quartered dumpling wrappers down on to a floured surface but keep them covered with a damp tea towel to stop them drying out.
3. Lightly wet the edges of a wrapper with your finger and place ½ teaspoon of filling into each square, then grab one of the filled squares and bring the four corners up together. Pinch along the edges to seal, like a star. Repeat this for all the dumplings.
4. Bring a large saucepan of salted water to the boil, then reduce the heat to low and add the dumplings. Let them simmer for 6 minutes until cooked.
5. Meanwhile, combine the yoghurt, feta and garlic in a small bowl, mashing with a fork until relatively smooth. Set aside.
6. For the paprika butter, put all the ingredients, except the mint, into a small bowl, then microwave for 30 seconds. (Alternatively melt the ingredients in a small saucepan over a very low heat.)
7. When your dumplings are ready, transfer them to a serving bowl with a slotted spoon. Spoon the feta yoghurt over the dumplings, drizzle with paprika butter, sprinkle with chopped mint, and enjoy!

Lemongrass, Beef & Basil 'Cheat' Pan-Fried Buns

SERVES 2-3

I adore making bao – a type of filled bun from China – but because you traditionally use yeast in the recipe, they can take a while to make. So, this 'cheat' recipe takes a fraction of the time but doesn't compromise on fluffiness or flavour.

FOR THE DUMPLINGS

200g self-raising (self-rising) flour, plus extra for dusting
180g (6½oz) Greek yoghurt
200g (7oz) 20% fat beef mince (ground beef)
1 lemongrass stalk, bashed to release the flavour, then finely chopped
1 small red onion, finely chopped
2 garlic cloves, finely chopped or grated
2 tbsp finely chopped basil leaves, plus extra to garnish
1 tbsp sesame oil
2 tbsp light soy sauce
½ tbsp sugar
½ tsp ground black pepper

TO SERVE

Drizzle of vegetable oil
1 tbsp chilli oil (optional)

1. Put the self-raising flour and Greek yoghurt into a large bowl and stir together using chopsticks or a wooden spoon until the dough roughly comes together. Turn out on to a lightly floured surface and combine the dough for 30 seconds until a rough light dough forms – the dough shouldn't stick to your hands too much; if it does, add a sprinkling more flour. Return the ball of dough back to the bowl, cover with cling film (plastic wrap) and set aside for 5–10 minutes while you make the filling.

2. Put all the remaining ingredients into another bowl and gently stir with chopsticks or a fork until a rough paste forms. Set aside.

3. Turn the ball of dough out on to a floured surface and pierce a hole through the middle with your finger. Form it into a doughnut shape, slice to make a long log about 30cm (12in) long and then slice the log into 6 equal pieces. Roll each piece out into a circular wrapper about 1cm (½in) thick and 10cm (4in) in diameter. Sprinkle the wrappers with flour to keep them from sticking.

4. Place a spoonful of the filling into the centre of the wrapper, then pull the edges up and seal in an anticlockwise motion, pinching as you work your way around. Repeat this step for all the dumplings.

5. Place the dumplings on to little pieces of cut out parchment paper. Set up your metal or bamboo steamer over a high heat, then place the dumplings (on their sheets of paper) inside. Add the lid and steam for 12 minutes, then turn off the heat and leave to steam for a further 1 minute.

6. To give the dumplings a crispy underside, place a non-stick pan over a medium heat and drizzle with vegetable oil. Add your dumplings, pattern side up, and fry for 4 minutes, or until the undersides are golden and crispy. Remove from the pan and serve scattered with a little finely chopped basil and a drizzle of chilli oil (if using). Enjoy!

Leek & Aubergine Moon Pouches

SERVES 2-3

Oyaki is a staple street food dumpling in Japanese cuisine, specifically in the Nagano Prefecture – a landlocked area on the main island Honshu – known for its mountainous landscapes, bustling wildlife and unique architecture. This aubergine moon dumpling recipe is inspired by Oyaki, however, the traditional recipe uses fermented buckwheat dough for the wrappers, giving an earthy result.

2 tbsp vegetable oil

1 medium aubergine (eggplant), finely chopped

1 medium leek, rinsed and thinly sliced

2 garlic cloves, finely chopped or grated

3 tbsp light soy sauce

2 tbsp sesame oil

1 tbsp rice wine vinegar

2 tsp sugar

16–20 round dumpling wrappers (ensure they are vegan)

2 tbsp black and white sesame seeds

1. Place a large frying pan (skillet) over a medium heat and drizzle in a tablespoon of the oil. Add the chopped aubergine, leek and garlic and fry for 5 minutes until the leeks have softened, and then add 2 tablespoons of the light soy sauce, the sesame oil, rice wine vinegar and 1 teaspoon of the sugar. Stir frequently and fry for another 3 minutes until the vegetables have fully softened and dried out slightly. Taste and adjust the seasoning with more soy sauce, vinegar or sugar, if you think it needs it.

2. Next, get your dumpling wrappers out (make sure you keep them covered under a damp tea towel so they don't dry out). Working on one at a time, lightly wet the edges of a wrapper with your finger and add a heaped teaspoon of the filling into the centre. Bring all the edges of the dumpling wrapper up to the centre, then pinch to seal. Flip over, and lightly pat down to make a thick, round, flat dumpling.

3. Tip the black and white sesame seeds on to a plate. One by one, brush the neat side of the dumpling with water and then dunk into the sesame seeds, covering one side of the dumpling. Set aside and repeat with the other dumplings.

4. Place a non-stick frying pan over a medium heat and drizzle with the remaining tablespoon of oil. Gently add the dumplings, sesame seed side down into the pan. Fry for 2 minutes, or until slightly golden, then reduce the heat to low and flip on to the other side.

5. Pour 50ml (generous 2½fl oz) water, the remaining soy sauce and sugar into the pan, then cover with a lid and leave to steam for 6 minutes.

6. Remove the lid to let any leftover water evaporate, then plate up the dumplings and enjoy!

Dough Clusters in a Creamy Kimchi, Bacon & Broccoli Stew

SERVES 2-3

Being obsessed with the spicy, tangy flavour of kimchi, I came up with this perfectly balanced, creamy bacon, broccoli and kimchi stew with Hungarian nokedli. Similar to German spaetzle, they are great little dumplings – the unctuous stew and doughy clusters are honestly a match made in heaven.

FOR THE DUMPLINGS

150g (generous 5oz) plain (all-purpose) flour
½ tsp salt
2 eggs, lightly beaten
2 tbsp sour cream
40ml (1½fl oz) milk (you may need more or less)

FOR THE SAUCE

2 tbsp olive oil
4 thinly sliced rashers of bacon, chopped into pieces
150g (generous 5oz) broccoli florets, roughly chopped into small pieces
1 tbsp gochujang
1 tsp sugar
300ml (10fl oz) single (light) cream
1 tsp ground black pepper
30g (1oz) grated Parmesan cheese
2 spring onions (scallions), finely chopped
100g (3½oz) kimchi
1 tbsp sesame seeds

1. Sift the flour and salt into a bowl, add the eggs and sour cream and combine thoroughly. Gradually add the milk until you have a soft dough that is sticky, but not runny.

2. Bring a saucepan of salted water to the boil, then reduce the heat to a simmer. Tip the dough out on to a wet chopping board (this stops the dough sticking to the board); then using the back of a knife, slice off small dumplings and scrape them into the pan of boiling water. You could also use the back of large spatula for this and then scrape small strings of the dough into the water.

3. When you're done scraping all of the dough into the pan, leave the dumplings to cook for a further 30 seconds, or until they've floated to the top. Remove with a slotted spoon, transfer to a plate and set aside.

4. Meanwhile, heat the olive oil in a non-stick frying pan (skillet) over a medium heat and add the bacon and broccoli. Fry for 5 minutes, stirring frequently, then reduce the heat to low. Stir in the gochujang, sugar, cream and black pepper, taste and adjust the seasoning, then add the dumplings to the creamy sauce. Give everything a mix.

5. Transfer the dumplings to serving bowls or plates. Sprinkle over the grated Parmesan, spring onions, kimchi and sesame seeds and serve. Enjoy!

Open-ended Chipotle Pork & Aubergine Parcels

SERVES 2-3

Even if you aren't hugely clued up on Mexican cuisine, chances are you've heard of chipotle. These dumplings are a wonderful amalgamation of Mexican-style flavours and Chinese-inspired dumpling style. They're really simple to fold and assemble, so do give them a go!

FOR THE STEW

Drizzle of olive oil
½ red onion, chopped
1 garlic clove, finely chopped or grated
1 tbsp chipotle paste
1 tbsp tomato purée
1 tsp ground cumin
400g (14oz) tin kidney beans, drained and rinsed
½ x 400g (14oz) tin chopped tomatoes
200ml (7fl oz) vegetable stock
Sea salt and black pepper

FOR THE DUMPLINGS

200g (7oz) pork mince (ground pork)
100g (3½oz) aubergine (eggplant), finely chopped
1 garlic clove, finely chopped or grated
1 tbsp chipotle paste
1 tbsp tomato purée
1 tsp ground cumin
16–20 round dumpling wrappers
1 tbsp olive oil

TO SERVE

1 ripe avocado, mashed
5 cherry tomatoes, finely chopped
½ red onion, finely chopped
Juice of ½ lime (cut the other half into wedges)
Coriander (cilantro) leaves

1. Heat the olive oil in a saucepan over a medium heat and add the chopped red onion and garlic. Fry for a minute before adding the chipotle paste, tomato purée, ground cumin, 1 teaspoon sea salt and 1 teaspoon black pepper. Fry for another minute.

2. Pour in the kidney beans, tinned tomatoes and vegetable stock and bring to the boil, then reduce the heat to low and leave to simmer while you make the dumplings, stirring from time to time. Taste and adjust the seasoning.

3. In a large bowl, combine the pork mince, aubergine, garlic, chipotle paste, tomato purée, cumin and a teaspoon each of sea salt and black pepper. Mix thoroughly until a chunky paste forms.

4. Next, get your dumpling wrappers out (keep them covered under a damp tea towel so they don't dry out) and one by one, lightly wet the edges of the dumpling wrappers with your finger. Add a heaped teaspoon of the filling into the centre of the wrapper. Bring up the two of the sides of the wrapper and pinch together to form a little basket-style bag. Repeat with the rest of the wrappers and filling.

5. Heat the oil in a large non-stick frying pan (skillet) over a medium heat. Gently place the dumplings into the pan (in batches if necessary, or use two frying pans!) and fry for 2 minutes. Pour in 60ml (2fl oz) water, reduce the heat to low and cover with a lid. Cook for 6 minutes, then remove the lid to let the remaining water evaporate.

6. Meanwhile, combine the avocado, tomatoes, red onion and lime juice in a bowl, season with salt and pepper and give it a taste.

7. To serve, ladle the bean stew into shallow bowls and top with the dumplings. Finish with spoonfuls of avocado crush, a few coriander leaves and a wedge of lime. Enjoy!

Three-ingredient Dumplings in a Three-ingredient Sauce

SERVES 2-3

There are countless versions of this dish throughout the Dominican Republic, where it is known as Dominican domplines. These doughy dumplings are the ultimate comfort food, especially when they soak up all the flavours of the sauce. Now, don't be put off by the chewiness of these dumplings because they're genuinely so delicious; I can easily devour a bowl and always go back for more.

FOR THE DOUGH
250g (9oz) plain (all-purpose) flour
50g (scant 2oz) room temperature butter, diced
1 tsp flaky sea salt

FOR THE SAUCE
1 red (bell) pepper, roughly chopped
200ml (7fl oz) single (light) cream
1 tsp flaky sea salt
½ tsp ground black pepper
70g (2½oz) Cheddar cheese, grated
Chopped fresh parsley, to garnish

1. Tip the flour into a large bowl and add the butter. Using your fingertips, rub the butter into the flour until it's completely combined with the flour, then add 100ml (3½fl oz) water and the salt. Knead for 30 seconds – you should have a dough that doesn't stick to your hands, but you can still feel the butteriness and moisture. Cover the bowl and place in the fridge while you make the sauce.
2. Add the red pepper, cream, salt and pepper to a blender and blitz until smooth, then transfer to a saucepan and place over a low heat. Add the grated Cheddar and cook, stirring, until it thickens slightly. Taste and adjust the seasoning.
3. Remove the dough from the fridge and tear it into small, bite-sized pieces. One by one, roll them into worm-like strips around 8cm (3in) long in the palms of your hands. You want the middle of the dumpling to be thicker than the ends. Repeat the process until the dough is used up.
4. Bring a large saucepan of salted water to the boil. Gently lower in the dumplings and let them simmer for 3 minutes, then use a slotted spoon to transfer the dumplings from the boiling water into the sauce. Combine gently so that the dumplings are coated in the sauce.
5. Serve up into bowls and sprinkle with the parsley.

Chorizo Butter Bean Dumplings with Tomatoes, Anchovies & Olives

To anyone who says beans are bland, please just try this recipe and then get back to me. Beans are a robust ingredient that help carry flavour and boost texture, plus they are just really good for you. This recipe was inspired by my infectiously joyful friend, Tats, saying how fun it would be to have a dumpling that reminded us of a classic Mediterranean holiday with fresh flavours, hints of heat and tart feta. The result: chorizo butter bean dumplings on a bed of zingy tomato sauce with anchovies and olives. And an absolute feast for the senses.

FOR THE DUMPLINGS

½ red onion, roughly chopped
1 garlic clove
½ red (bell) pepper, roughly chopped
150g (generous 5oz) chorizo, roughly chopped
150g (generous 5oz) tinned/jarred butter beans
16–20 square dumpling wrappers

FOR THE SAUCE

2 tbsp olive oil
2 garlic cloves, finely chopped or grated
4 anchovy fillets
10 pitted olives, roughly chopped
2 tbsp tomato purée
400g (14oz) tinned tomatoes
1 tsp paprika
½ tsp sugar
Salt and pepper

TO SERVE

100g (3½oz) feta cheese, crumbled
Basil leaves, roughly torn

1. Start by preparing the sauce. Heat the olive oil in a large, non-stick frying pan (skillet) over a low heat. Add the garlic, anchovy fillets, olives and tomato purée and fry for 2 minutes, stirring frequently to break up the anchovy fillets.

2. Pour in the tinned tomatoes, paprika and sugar and season to taste with salt and pepper (you won't need much salt as the anchovies and olives are already quite salty). Leave to simmer over a low heat while you make the dumplings.

3. Put the red onion, garlic clove, red pepper, chorizo, butter beans and some salt and pepper into a food processor and blitz until a rough paste forms.

4. Next, get your dumpling wrappers out (but keep them covered under a damp tea towel so they don't dry out). Working on one at a time, lightly wet the edges of a dumpling wrapper with your finger and add a heaped teaspoon of the filling to the centre of the wrapper. Fold the wrapper in half to make a triangle and pinch to seal. Make sure you press against the filling when sealing to remove any air and seal really tightly so there are no gaps. Repeat for all the dumplings, keeping the sealed dumplings under a damp tea towel.

5. Bring a large saucepan of salted water to the boil, then reduce the heat to a simmer and gently lower in your dumplings. Cook for 3 minutes, then drain.

6. Divide the sauce between plates, followed by the dumplings. Scatter over the crumbled feta and basil and enjoy!

Air Fryer Crab Rangoon

SERVES 2–3

You'll find variations of crab rangoon across the US as they are a popular appetiser in American-Chinese restaurants. Filled with a creamy, cheesy, tangy imitation crab meat (crabstick) filling, they're then encased in square wonton wrappers and typically deep-fried. I've chosen to air fry them for a healthier and easier alternative, but if you don't have an air fryer they can easily be deep-fried in a saucepan of hot sunflower oil for 6 minutes, or until golden. Served with sweet chilli sauce, they're a great appetiser for when you're looking to entertain a crowd.

150g (generous 5oz) imitation crab meat (crab sticks), shredded

150g (generous 5oz) cream cheese

30g (1oz) grated Cheddar cheese

1 garlic clove, finely chopped or grated

1 tbsp mayonnaise

1 tbsp Worcestershire sauce

Juice of ½ lemon

1 tbsp sriracha

1 tsp paprika

16–20 square wrappers (wonton)

Vegetable oil, for brushing

TO SERVE

1 spring onion (scallion), thinly sliced

3 tbsp sweet chilli sauce

1. In a bowl, combine the crab meat, cream cheese, grated Cheddar, garlic, mayonnaise, Worcestershire sauce, lemon juice, sriracha and paprika. Stir to mix well. Taste and adjust the seasoning accordingly.

2. Lay out the wonton wrappers on your work surface (but keep them covered under a damp tea towel so they don't dry out) and brush the edges with water.

3. Place a heaped teaspoon of the filling into the centre of each wrapper. Bring each corner of the square up into the centre and seal along the sides, pushing out any air inside the wrapper. You should have a little kite-shaped dumpling. Now grab two 'points' of the star and pinch them together, then do the same on the other side. Your dumpling should now look like binoculars.

4. Brush the dumplings with oil and place in the air fryer basket, making sure there is enough space around them (cook in batches if necessary).

5. Air fry for 10 minutes at 180°C/350°F, flipping them over halfway through cooking.

6. To serve, scatter the crab rangoon with sliced spring onion and serve with sweet chilli sauce for dipping.

Twist on a Reuben

SERVES 2-3

The Reuben: an absolute classic North American grilled sandwich consisting of corned beef, Swiss cheese, sauerkraut and a saucy dressing wedged in between slices of rye bread. I love it. I also love käsknöpfle, a traditional cheese dumpling dish from Liechtenstein, so I thought it was time to get experimental and combine the two dishes. And what a result. This has to be one of the most comforting recipes in this book, yet with every bite you get an explosion of flavour.

FOR THE DUMPLINGS
250g (9oz) plain flour (all-purpose flour)
2 tsp flaky sea salt
2 medium eggs

FOR THE CARAMELIZED ONIONS
2 tbsp vegetable oil
1 white onion, thinly sliced
½ tbsp balsamic vinegar
Pinch of sugar
Salt and pepper

FOR THE SAUCE
100g (3½oz) Emmental cheese, grated
1 tbsp mayonnaise
½ tbsp tomato ketchup
2 tsp horseradish sauce
2 tsp hot sauce
1 tsp Worcestershire sauce
½ tsp paprika

TO SERVE
4 slices of salt beef, chopped
2–3 tbsp sauerkraut
2 dill pickles, finely chopped

1. Sift the flour and salt in a bowl, make a well in the centre and add the eggs and 150ml (5fl oz) water. Whisk until you have a smooth, thick batter – thicker than a pancake batter, but not as thick as a cake batter. The dough needs to be able to drop through the holes of a colander so if it looks too thick, add a little water until it reaches the right consistency. Cover and set aside while you prepare the caramelized onion.

2. Heat the oil in a frying pan (skillet) over a medium heat, add the sliced onion and fry for 10–15 minutes, stirring frequently, until caramelised. Add the balsamic vinegar and sugar and season with salt and pepper. Set aside.

3. Now to cook the dumplings. Bring a saucepan of salted water to the boil, then reduce to a simmer. Place a colander (or large-holed potato ricer) over the top of the saucepan, pour in the batter and push the dough through the holes of the colander using a spatula. The dough should fall in small droplets and form little balls in the water. Cook for 1 minute, or until they've floated to the surface. Drain and set aside in a large bowl.

4. Add all the sauce ingredients to the bowl of dumplings and give everything a mix until stringy, cheesy and well combined. Season with salt and pepper to taste.

5. Transfer to a serving plate, top with the caramelized onions and serve with sliced salt beef, sauerkraut and chopped pickles.

One-pot Spicy Beef Stew with Chilean-style Dumplings

SERVES 2–3

This is the kind of one-pot dish I go to when I'm looking for something simple but hearty. Chilean pantrucas – the inspiration for this dish – is a warming soup consisting of beef broth, flat dumplings and an assortment of meat and veggies. Despite never having lived in Chile (only visited – and fell in love with the place), this dish never fails to remind me of the flavours of my childhood: the warmth from the spice, the delicacy from the beef and the soft texture of the dumplings. Feel free to jazz it up or down by adjusting the flavourings based on your preferences.

FOR THE STEW

1 tbsp oil
1 onion, finely chopped
2 garlic cloves, finely chopped
   or grated
200g (7oz) beef mince (ground beef)
   – the higher the fat, the tastier the
   meat
1 carrot, julienned
1 red (bell) pepper, julienned
1 tsp dried oregano
1 tsp ground cumin
1 tsp smoked paprika
½ red chilli, finely chopped
1 tsp sugar
1 potato, cut into small cubes
1 litre (35floz) beef stock
Salt and pepper

FOR THE DUMPLINGS

150g (generous 5oz) plain
   (all-purpose) flour, plus extra
   for rolling
1 egg

TO SERVE

Sour cream
Finely chopped parsley
Lime wedges

1. Heat the oil in a large saucepan over a medium heat, add the onion and garlic and fry for 3 minutes until slightly softened and aromatic. Add the beef and fry for a further 3 minutes, until browned all over.

2. Add the carrot, red pepper, dried oregano, cumin, smoked paprika and chilli and fry for a further 3 minutes, stirring often, then stir in the sugar, diced potato and beef stock. Bring to the boil, then reduce the heat, cover with a lid and leave to simmer over a low heat for 10 minutes while you make the dumplings. Give it a stir every now and then and season to taste with salt and pepper and more chilli and/or sugar, if you think it needs it.

3. Combine the flour, egg and 2 tablespoons water in a large bowl until a rough dough forms – gently add more water if needed until the dough is play-dough in feel (firm but malleable), or add more flour if the dough is sticking to your hands. Knead in the bowl for 1 minute, then turn the dough out on to a floured surface and use a rolling pin to roll out to a thickness of about 3mm (⅛in). Slice the dough lengthways into strips 2.5cm (1in) wide, and then slice the strips into squares.

4. Add the dumpling squares to the stew and cook, uncovered, for 2 minutes, stirring very gently.

5. Serve the dumpling stew in deep bowls and top each with a dollop of sour cream, some chopped parsley and a lime wedge.

Miso Ragu & Scissor-cut Dumplings

SERVES 2-3

Scissor-cut dumplings (some may argue they're noodles) have been eaten in China for aeons and for good reason: they're ultra simple to make. All you need is your homemade two-ingredient dough and some scissors. I've chosen to pair the super chewy dumplings with one of my favourite types of ragu, miso ragu. Inspired by Japanese flavours, it's packed full of umami and has a slight sweetness to it. Finished with a sprinkle of Parmesan, chopped spring onions and chilli oil, it's a bowl of food I come back to again and again.

FOR THE DUMPLINGS
200g (7oz) plain (all-purpose) flour
½ tsp salt

FOR THE MISO RAGU
2 tbsp olive oil
1 onion, finely chopped
3 garlic cloves, finely chopped
  or grated
1 carrot, finely chopped
1 celery stick, finely chopped
200g (7oz) beef mince (ground beef)
1 tsp ground black pepper
1 tsp chilli flakes
½ tsp sugar
1 tbsp white miso paste
1 tsp rice wine vinegar
1 tbsp light soy sauce
2 tbsp tomato purée
400ml (13½fl oz) coconut milk
100ml (3½fl oz) beef stock
Salt and pepper

TO SERVE
2 spring onions (scallions), finely
  chopped
Black and/or white sesame seeds
1 tbsp grated Parmesan cheese
1 tbsp chilli oil

1. Start by making the dumpling dough: put the flour, salt and 100ml (3½fl oz) water into a large bowl and stir using chopsticks or a wooden spoon until the dough begins to clump up. Knead in the bowl for 1 minute until a rough dough forms (it doesn't need to look perfect). Cover the bowl with cling film (plastic wrap) and set aside in the fridge while you make the ragu.

2. Heat the oil in a large saucepan over a medium heat and add the onion, garlic, carrot and celery. Fry for 3 minutes until the vegetables have softened slightly, then add the beef mince, pepper, chilli flakes and sugar. Fry for 5 minutes, stirring often.

3. Add the miso paste, rice wine vinegar, soy sauce and tomato purée and give everything a good stir, then pour in the coconut milk and beef stock and bring to the boil. Reduce the heat and leave to simmer for 10 minutes.

4. Remove the rested dough from the fridge and knead it again for 30 seconds. Bring another large saucepan of salted water to the boil, then reduce the heat slightly so the water is at a gentle boil.

5. With the dough in one hand and scissors in the other, hold the dough over the pot and snip off small strips of dumpling. The strips should be about ½cm (¼in) thick and 2.5cm (1in) long. As you snip, allow them to fall into the water. Cook for 2 minutes, then drain and immediately add to your ragu. Stir until everything is well combined, then season to taste with salt and pepper.

6. Spoon the ragu and dumplings on to plates and serve scattered with chopped spring onion, sesame seeds, grated Parmesan and a drizzle of chilli oil. Enjoy!

Creamy 'Vori Vori' Dumpling Bowl

SERVES 2–3

I love eggs on pretty much anything ... fried, boiled, or poached. I just think they add an extra creaminess and textural angle that elevates any dish. This bowl of comfort food is a creamy take on Paraguayan vori vori (or bori bori) – a thick soup dotted with small maize flour and cheese balls. The dumplings themselves are pretty close to the traditional recipe (I've used grated mozzarella cheese instead of queso fresco), but the soup has more of a twist. You get the nutritional benefits of chickpeas and spinach combined with the comfort of a creamy chicken soup, along with the flavours of chilli and garlic. It's a hug in a bowl and great for a midweek supper.

FOR THE SOUP BOWL

2 tbsp olive oil
2 chicken breasts, cut into bite-sized chunks
2 garlic cloves, finely chopped or grated
400g (14oz) tinned/jarred chickpeas (garbanzo beans), drained and rinsed
30g (1oz) grated Parmesan cheese, plus extra to serve
300ml (10fl oz) single (light) cream
500ml (generous 1 pint) chicken stock
150g (generous 5oz) spinach
2–3 eggs, boiled for 6 minutes
1 red chilli, thinly sliced
Salt and pepper

FOR THE DUMPLINGS

160g (5½oz) fine pre-cooked maize flour (I used the brand PAN)
70g (2½oz) grated mozzarella cheese
1 tsp salt
1 tsp paprika
200ml (7fl oz) milk

1. Heat 1 tablespoon of the oil in a frying pan (skillet) over a medium heat and add the chicken pieces. Fry for 5 minutes, stirring often, then add the garlic, chickpeas, grated Parmesan and 1 teaspoon of black pepper. Fry for 1 minute.

2. Add the single cream and chicken stock, stir and bring to a simmer. Season to taste with salt and pepper. Leave to simmer for 10 minutes, stirring occasionally, while you prepare the dumplings.

3. Add the maize flour, cheese, salt and paprika to a large bowl and stir to combine. Gradually stir in the milk until a slightly moist dough forms that you can roll into 2.5cm (1in) balls. Roll the dumplings in the palm of your hand to form seamless soft balls. Optionally, toss them in a bit more maize flour to seal, then set aside. Repeat for all the dumplings.

4. Bring a saucepan of salted water to the boil, then reduce the heat to medium. Gently lower in the dough balls and simmer over a low heat for 3–4 minutes.

5. Meanwhile, add the spinach to the pan of creamy chicken and let it wilt.

6. Remove the cooked dumplings from the pan with a slotted spoon and add to the chicken, then spoon the creamy chicken and dumplings into bowls. Top with the halved medium-boiled eggs, grated Parmesan and thinly sliced red chillies. Enjoy!

Cauliflower & Mushroom Dough Balls with a Tomato & Walnut Ragu

SERVES 2–3 These Alpine balls of joy take me back to when we travelled to the Dolomites in Italy. We were in a glass-fronted restaurant perched on the side of Seceda Mountain, munching on canederli – milky bread dumplings typically filled with local cured meats and cheese. They're the epitome of comfort, especially on a cold winter's day. I've omitted the local cured meats and opted for the more veg-focused cauliflower and mushroom combo.

FOR THE DUMPLINGS

200g (7oz) bread, roughly chopped into 1–2cm (½–1in) pieces
100g (3½oz) cauliflower florets
100g (3½oz) mushrooms
2 tbsp (10g or scant ½oz) finely chopped parsley, plus extra to garnish
100g (3½oz) Gouda cheese, finely chopped
½ white onion, roughly chopped
30g (1oz) plain (all-purpose) flour, plus extra for dusting
1 tsp each salt and black pepper
1 garlic clove, minced
1 egg
1 tbsp milk
1 tbsp olive oil

FOR THE WALNUT RAGU

100g (3½oz) walnuts
1 carrot, roughly chopped
1 celery stick, roughly chopped
4 garlic cloves
½ white onion
2 tbsp dried mixed herbs
2 tbsp olive oil
2 tbsp tomato purée
400g (14oz) tomato passata
100ml (3fl oz) vegetable stock
½ tbsp balsamic vinegar
Salt and pepper

1. Add all the dumpling ingredients except for the egg, milk and olive oil to a food processor and blitz until everything is roughly chopped. Transfer the mixture to a large bowl (don't wash out the processor as you will be using it again), add the remaining dumpling ingredients and combine thoroughly with your hands until you have a dough. If the dough is sticking to your hands a lot, add a little more flour. It should look uniformly moist and slightly sticky. Cover the bowl and set aside while you prepare the ragu.

2. Add the walnuts, carrot, celery, garlic, onion and mixed herbs to the food processor bowl and blitz until finely chopped.

3. Place a frying pan (skillet) over a medium heat and drizzle with the olive oil. Pour in the walnut mixture and fry for 5 minutes, stirring occasionally, then add the remaining ragu ingredients and season with salt and pepper. Leave to simmer until your dumplings are ready. Taste and adjust the seasoning.

4. Meanwhile, divide the dough into 12 portions and then use your hands to roll each one into a ball just bigger than a golf ball. Roll each ball in flour to seal the outside.

5. Bring a large saucepan of salted water to the boil. Using a slotted spoon, gently lower in your dumplings and leave them to simmer for 12 minutes.

6. When the dumplings are ready, spoon the walnut ragu into serving bowls and top with the juicy dumplings and chopped parsley. Enjoy!

Pea & Ricotta Squares with Crispy Prosciutto

SERVES 2

This pea and ricotta combo topped with crispy prosciutto is a great way to demonstrate the beauty of ravioli. I've taken a handy shortcut here, using store-bought square wonton wrappers to envelop our simple yet refreshing pea and ricotta filling (although you can make your own if you have more time). Plus there's no need for a sauce with this because you've got enough moisture from the filling; just serve with a little butter, dollops of extra ricotta and salty prosciutto. It's honestly a great way to enter your ravioli-making era ... and a great way to impress friends and family.

FOR THE DUMPLINGS

200g (7oz) peas
150g (generous 5oz) ricotta cheese
1 garlic clove, finely chopped or grated
2 tbsp grated Parmesan cheese
16–20 square wonton wrappers
Salt and pepper

TO SERVE

1 tbsp olive oil
4 slices of Prosciutto
50g (scant 2oz) frozen peas, defrosted
1 tbsp butter
2 tbsp ricotta

1. Tip the peas into a large bowl and mash them lightly with the back of a fork, then add the ricotta, garlic, grated Parmesan and a big pinch of salt and pepper. Combine thoroughly.

2. Get your dumpling wrappers out but keep them covered with a damp tea towel so they don't dry out while you assemble the ravioli.

3. Line up 8–10 square wrappers on a clean surface and place a heaped teaspoon of the filling into the centre of each square. Lightly wet the edges of the wrappers with water using your finger. Then, top each filling with another dumpling wrapper, gently pressing down around the filling to remove any air bubbles and sealing to form a square ravioli. If they look a bit messy, feel free to use a sharp knife to trim them into neater squares.

4. Bring a saucepan of salted water to the boil, then reduce the heat to a gentle simmer. Carefully lower in the ravioli and simmer for 4 minutes.

5. Meanwhile, heat the olive oil in a non-stick frying pan (skillet) over a high heat. Add slices of prosciutto and fry for 2 minutes on each side, or until crispy. Remove from the pan and chop into rough pieces.

6. Add the peas to a small bowl and microwave for 2 minutes. (Alternatively, boil them in a small saucepan.)

7. When your ravioli are cooked, remove with a slotted spoon and divide between your plates. Top each plate with ½ tablespoon of butter, then scatter over the peas, dollops of ricotta and the pieces of fried prosciutto.

Buffalo Chicken Triangles with a Blue Cheese Sauce

SERVES 2–3

The flavour of this dish is unique, with a subtle hint of chilli and lots of earthiness from the blue cheese; add to that the lime, jalapeños, chives and extra dosage of buffalo sauce and it's the kind of dish that you can wolf down in one sitting. The flavours are inspired by the classic buffalo chicken wing, a much-loved dish served throughout the US. I discovered that barbecue sauce is a great substitute for those who aren't great chilli fans, transforming the dish into a sweeter, smokier result that works just as well as the buffalo version.

FOR THE DUMPLINGS

200g (7oz) chicken mince (ground chicken)
1 celery stick, finely diced
1 small carrot, grated
½ red onion, finely chopped
2 tbsp buffalo sauce (or barbecue sauce)
2 tbsp finely chopped parsley
16–20 round dumpling wrappers
Salt and pepper

FOR THE SAUCE

50g (scant 2oz) blue cheese (I use Saint Agur)
2 tbsp sour cream
1 tbsp mayonnaise
1 tbsp milk

TO SERVE

2 tbsp buffalo sauce (or barbecue sauce)
Finely chopped chives
Jarred jalapeños, thinly sliced
Lime wedges

1. Combine the chicken, celery, carrot, red onion, buffalo sauce and parsley in a large bowl and season with salt and pepper. Mix until well combined.
2. Next, get your dumpling wrappers out (keep them covered under a damp tea towel so they don't dry out). Working on one at a time, lightly wet the edges of a dumpling wrapper with your finger and add a heaped teaspoon of the filling to the centre of the wrapper. Bring the three sides of the circle up into the centre and lightly pinch together, then seal along the three edges. Repeat for all the dumplings, keeping the sealed dumplings under a damp tea towel.
3. Prepare a steamer and place the dumplings in the steamer basket. Steam for 6–8 minutes.
4. Meanwhile, combine all the ingredients for the sauce in a bowl. Pour the buffalo sauce for serving into a separate bowl.
5. Once the dumplings are cooked, toss them in the buffalo sauce until coated. Add your blue cheese sauce to the base of each plate and divide the coated dumplings between plates. Scatter with chives, jalapeño slices and serve with a wedge of lime.

SERVES 2–3

Rice Noodles, Crispy Air Fryer Dumplings & a Green Dressing

This recipe doesn't have a specific origin, but there are major influences from China for the mini spring roll dumplings and Vietnam for the flat rice noodles and green herby aromatic dressing. I've chosen to air fry these 'spring rolls' but you could also deep-fry them, or even steam them (for about 7 minutes) if you're looking for a softer result.

FOR THE DUMPLINGS

2 garlic cloves, finely chopped
  or grated
200g (7oz) pork mince (ground pork)
1 carrot, grated
50g (scant 2oz) beansprouts
2 tbsp oyster sauce
16 square dumpling wrappers
Vegetable oil, for brushing

FOR THE DRESSING

30g (1oz) coriander (cilantro) leaves
15g (½oz) mint leaves
1 small garlic clove
1 green chilli
½ tbsp sugar
½ tsp salt
Juice of 1 lime
4 tbsp vegetable oil

FOR THE DISH

200g (7oz) dried rice noodles
½ cucumber, thinly julienned
1 carrot, peeled to create thin strips
1 red chilli, thinly sliced
2 spring onions (scallions), thinly
  sliced
Small handful of mint, roughly
  chopped
Small handful of coriander (cilantro),
  roughly chopped
Small handful of peanuts, lightly
  bashed (optional)

1. In a large bowl, combine all the dumpling ingredients (except the wrappers) and mix together until you have a rough paste.

2. Get your wrappers out but keep them covered with a damp tea towel so they don't dry out. Place one wrapper in a diamond position facing you and lightly wet the edges with a finger. Place a heaped spoonful of the filling at the bottom of the wrapper. Roll up halfway, then fold the sides into the centre and finish rolling. Seal and set aside while you repeat for the remaining dumplings.

3. Place the dumplings in the air fryer, brush with vegetable oil and cook at 180°C/350°F for 12 minutes, turning halfway, until golden and crispy.

4. Meanwhile, cook or soak your rice noodles according to the packet instructions. Drain and rinse under cold water to keep them springy. Prepare the rest of your ingredients.

5. In a blender, whizz together all the dressing ingredients with 4 tablespoons water. Taste and adjust the seasoning; you can also add more oil or water if the sauce isn't the right thickness for you.

6. To serve, spread the tangy green sauce out on to a serving platter. Add the rice noodles and top with cucumber, carrot, red chilli and spring onions. Scatter over the fresh herbs and peanuts, if using, and finish with your crispy dumplings. Enjoy!

Peri Peri Chicken Boats with Burrata

SERVES 2

I'm not one to have favourites, but this dish has to be up there if you're looking to go to flavour town. Inspired by the style and design of Armenian dumplings (manti) and the wonderfully spicy Mozambique/Portuguese peri peri (a sauce with a slightly controversial origin story), this dish will wow you with every bite. The sauce is easy to whip up, and using pre-made wrappers simplifies the dumpling-making process. Once assembled, the plate is topped with creamy burrata to cool some of the heat and parsley for freshness.

FOR THE DUMPLINGS
400g (14oz) chicken mince (ground chicken)
½ small onion, finely chopped
2 tsp peri peri seasoning or paprika
12–16 square wrappers
Salt and pepper

FOR THE SAUCE
1 red (bell) pepper
½–1 red chilli, to taste, or leave out if you don't like chilli
2 garlic cloves
1 tbsp dried oregano
100ml (3½fl oz) olive oil
½ tbsp smoked paprika
Juice of ½ lemon
½ teaspoon sugar

TO FINISH
1 ball of burrata
Chopped parsley

1. Combine the chicken, onion and peri peri seasoning in a bowl and season with salt and pepper. Give it all a good mix.
2. Get your wrappers out but keep them under a damp tea towel to stop them drying out. Working on one at a time, place 2 heaped teaspoons of the filling into the centre of a wrapper.
   Wet the edges of the wrappers with your finger, then fold two corners up together on one side and pinch together. Repeat on the other side, leaving the filling uncovered in the middle (it should look like a boat with the filling as the middle). Repeat this for all the dumplings.
3. Once the dumplings are ready, prepare a steamer and steam the dumplings for 8 minutes.
4. Meanwhile, add all the sauce ingredients, except for the sugar, to a blender and whizz into a smooth sauce. Add the sugar and stir. Transfer the sauce to a heatproof bowl and heat up in the microwave for 3 minutes until piping hot (or heat in a small saucepan over a low heat).
5. Once your dumplings are ready, divide the hot peri peri sauce between two plates as the base. Top with the dumplings, then tear over the burrata and scatter with parsley. Enjoy!

A BIT MORE EFFORT

30+MINS

MAXIMUM

Some of these recipes require a little bit more time, and a teeny bit more effort. But honestly, they're so delicious and are all absolute crowd-pleasers.

SATIS FACTION

Greek Beans Topped with Parmesan Dumplings

Gigantes plaki – literally translating as giant baked beans – is a hearty and wholesome dish eaten throughout Greece. As baked beans are so popular in the UK, I thought why not combine these baked butter beans with the British classic, suet dumplings. The result is a perfect pairing of warming flavours and comforting textures.

FOR THE BAKED BEANS

2 tbsp olive oil
½ onion, finely chopped
1 carrot, finely chopped
1 leek, thinly sliced
3 garlic cloves, finely chopped
   or grated
½ tbsp dried thyme
½ tbsp dried oregano
1 tsp red pepper flakes
400g (14oz) tin chopped tomatoes
200ml (7fl oz) vegetable stock
400g (14oz) tin butter beans,
   drained and rinsed
Bunch of parsley, roughly chopped
200g (7oz) feta cheese, crumbled
   (optional)
Salt and pepper

FOR THE DUMPLINGS

150g (generous 5oz) self-raising
   (self-rising) flour
½ tsp fine salt
70g (½oz) shredded suet (or use
   diced butter)
50g Parmesan cheese, grated
150ml (5fl oz) milk

1. Preheat the oven to 200°C/400°F.
2. Heat the olive oil in a large frying pan (skillet) over a medium heat and add the onion, carrot, leek and garlic. Season with salt and pepper and cook, stirring frequently, for 5 minutes until the vegetables soften.
3. Add the dried thyme, oregano and pepper flakes and fry for another minute before adding the chopped tomatoes, stock and butter beans. Cook for a further 5 minutes, then taste and adjust the seasoning with more salt, pepper or a pinch of sugar.
4. Meanwhile, to make the dumplings, put the flour, salt and suet into a bowl and rub the suet into the flour with your fingertips until it resembles fine breadcrumbs. Stir in the Parmesan and gradually pour in the milk, combining with a spoon until you have a soft, sticky dough. Divide into 8 balls.
5. Transfer the beans to a lidded ovenproof dish and arrange the dumplings on top. Cover, put into the oven and bake for 20 minutes, then remove the lid and cook for a further 15 minutes until the dumplings have doubled in size and are golden brown.
6. Scatter the chopped parsley and feta cheese, if using, over the dish and enjoy!

Crispy Bean Fritters with Sweet Chilli Cavolo Nero & Chickpea Stew

SERVES 2–3

This dish has it all: sweetness, vibrancy and a perfect kick from the jalapeños. The inspiration for this recipe stems from West African koose – spicy bean cakes – also known as akara and kosai. It's a popular street food and typically made with black-eyed peas. For this recipe, we're using butter beans for a creamy touch.

FOR THE DUMPLINGS

200g (7oz) jarred butter beans, drained and rinsed
½ onion, roughly chopped
2.5cm (1in) piece of ginger, finely chopped
1 garlic clove
1 fresh red chilli
1 tsp salt
100g (3½oz) self-raising (self-rising) flour
1½ tsp baking powder
Vegetable oil, for frying

FOR THE CHICKPEA AND CAVOLO NERO STEW

1 tbsp olive oil
½ onion, finely chopped
2 garlic cloves, finely chopped or grated
2 tbsp tomato purée
150g (generous 5oz) cavolo nero, stalks discarded, leaves roughly chopped
200g (7oz) tinned/jarred chickpeas (garbanzo beans), drained and rinsed
200g (7oz) tinned chopped tomatoes
200ml (7fl oz) vegetable stock
1 tbsp sweet chilli sauce
1 tbsp malt vinegar
Salt and pepper

TO GARNISH

50g (scant 2oz) grated Cheddar cheese
Jarred jalapeño slices

1. Add the butter beans to a food processor with the onion, ginger, garlic, chilli and a pinch of salt and blend until smooth. Transfer to a large bowl and add the self-raising flour, baking powder and 50ml (generous 2½fl oz) water. Combine until you have a smooth but thick batter. Set aside in the fridge while you make the stew.

2. Heat the olive oil in a saucepan over a medium heat and add the onion and garlic. Fry and stir for a few minutes until the onion has softened, then stir in the tomato purée, followed by the cavolo nero, chickpeas, tomatoes and vegetable stock. Bring to the boil and then reduce the heat to a simmer. Add the sweet chilli sauce and malt vinegar and season with salt and pepper. Leave to simmer over a low heat while you make your dumplings.

3. Pour vegetable oil into a medium saucepan to a depth of about 8–10cm (3–4in) and place over a medium heat. Test if the oil is ready by placing the handle of a wooden spoon into the oil to touch the base of the pan. If bubbles form around the base of the spoon handle, the oil is hot enough.

4. Using a tablespoon, scoop spoonfuls of the batter into the oil. Cook in batches of 3 or 4 to avoid overcrowding the pan. You will see them puff up into balls. Fry for 3–4 minutes, turning often to ensure they're evenly golden. Once cooked, remove using a slotted spoon and drain on a plate lined with kitchen paper (kitchen towel).

5. Ladle the stew into bowls and top with grated cheese, jalapeño slices and your bean dumpling fritters. Enjoy!

Cumin Pork Dumplings with Homemade Chilli Oil

SERVES 2–3

My love affair with homemade chilli dip began when I had my first plate of proper Chinese dumplings in Guangzhou. Most jiaozi (a type of Chinese dumpling) are served with a soy and vinegar dipping sauce that is sweet and tangy – perfect with little pockets of joy – but, for those who like a bit of a kick with their dumplings, you can't go wrong with a homemade chilli dip. It's also very, very easy to make; once you've bought the ingredients, it takes less than 5 minutes to rustle up.

FOR THE DUMPLINGS

1 tsp ground cumin

200g (7oz) pork mince (ground pork)

1 egg

2 tbsp Chinese Shaoxing wine

2 tbsp light soy sauce

1cm (½in) piece of ginger, grated

2 garlic cloves, finely chopped
    or grated

2 spring onions (scallions), thinly
    sliced

16–20 round dumpling wrappers

Drizzle of vegetable oil

FOR THE HOMEMADE CHILLI DIP

100ml (3½ fl oz) vegetable oil

2 garlic cloves, finely chopped
    or grated

1 lemongrass stick, top and tailed,
    bashed and finely chopped

1 tbsp sesame seeds

2 spring onions (scallions), finely
    chopped

½ tbsp sugar

1 tbsp chilli powder (I used finely
    ground gochugaru)

½ tsp salt

1. Combine all the dumpling ingredients (except the wrappers and oil) in a large bowl. Mix thoroughly until a paste forms.

2. Get your dumpling wrappers out but keep them covered under a damp tea towel so they don't dry out. One at a time, lightly wet the edges of a dumpling wrapper with your finger and add a heaped teaspoon of the filling to the centre of the wrapper. Fold the wrapper over the filling and pinch at the top of the semicircle with your fingers, but don't seal it yet.

3. Holding the wrapper in your left hand and starting near the top centre, fold a pleat on the top half of the wrapper using the thumb and index finger of your right hand; the pleat should turn towards the centre. Use your left thumb and index finger to press the folded pleat tightly against the back half of the wrapper. Repeat this along the right side, making 3–4 pleats. (For an easier quicker process, pinch and seal in the centre and then fold one pleat on each side of the dumpling, both facing inwards towards the centre – there are links to dumpling folding videos on pages 32–33)

4. Repeat on the left side of the dumpling, making 3–4 pleats with your left hand, all facing towards the centre. Press the pleats one last time to seal and then shape the dumpling to create a flat side on the bottom. Repeat with the remaining wrappers and filling to make all your dumplings.

CONTINUES OVERLEAF

CONTINUES
FROM PAGE 94

TO GARNISH

1 spring onion (scallion), thinly sliced
1 tsp sesame seeds

5. Place a non-stick frying pan (skillet) over a medium heat, drizzle in a little oil and add the dumplings. Fry for 2 minutes and then pour in 4 tablespoons water. Cover the pan with a lid and cook for 6 minutes.

6. Meanwhile, make your homemade chilli oil. Pour the oil into a saucepan and place over a low-medium heat. Add the garlic, lemongrass, sesame seeds and spring onions and fry for about 30 seconds, then turn off the heat. Stir in the sugar and chilli powder and then leave to cool.

7. Once your dumplings are nice and crispy, transfer them on to a serving plate. Drizzle with your homemade chilli oil, spring onions and sesame seeds and enjoy!

Chipotle Chicken & Corn Ball Casserole

SERVES 4

This is my version of North American Chicken and Dumplings but with all the punch and vibrancy you'd associate with Mexican flavours. You've got a quick and simple chipotle chicken creamy stew with the addition of carrots, celery and peas, topped with fluffy corn dumplings.

FOR THE STEW

2 tbsp olive oil
400g (14oz) skinless chicken breast or thigh fillets, roughly chopped
3 tbsp butter
½ red onion, diced
2 carrots, diced
1 celery stick, diced
3 garlic cloves, finely chopped or grated
1 tsp ground cumin
1 tsp dried oregano
2 tbsp chipotle paste
150ml (5fl oz) single (light) cream
500ml (generous 1 pint) chicken stock
2 tbsp plain (all-purpose) flour
150g (generous 5oz) frozen peas
Salt and pepper

FOR THE DUMPLINGS

200g (7oz) self-raising (self-rising) flour
1 tsp salt
1 tsp sugar
50g (scant 2oz) sour cream
100ml (3½fl oz) milk
2 tbsp melted butter
150g (generous 5oz) tinned sweetcorn, drained

TO GARNISH

Roughly chopped coriander (cilantro)
½ red onion, thinly sliced
Lime wedges

1. Heat the olive oil in a deep-sided frying pan (skillet) or casserole with a lid over a medium heat. Add the chicken pieces followed by a pinch of salt and a sprinkle of pepper and fry for 3 minutes until seared and golden.

2. Add the butter, red onion, carrots, celery, garlic, cumin and oregano and fry for 5 minutes, stirring frequently, until the vegetables have softened. Add the chipotle paste, followed by the single cream, chicken stock, flour and peas. Give everything a good mix and then cook for a further 10 minutes. You want the sauce to thicken slightly before adding in the dumplings, so if it's still quite runny, add in a couple more tablespoons of flour and cook until thickened. Taste and adjust the seasoning.

3. Meanwhile, make your dumplings. Tip the flour, salt and sugar into a large bowl and combine briefly, then add the sour cream, milk, butter and corn. Mix gently using a spoon just until everything is well incorporated – don't overmix or the dumplings will become dense! You're looking for a reasonably sticky dough.

4. Use two large spoons and scoop small balls of the mixture carefully over the casserole in an even layer (you should get about 8 dumplings). Cover the dish tightly with foil or a lid and leave to simmer over a low heat for 15 minutes. Don't lift the lid, as the dumplings need to steam.

5. After 15 minutes, lift the lid and insert a wooden skewer into the middle of a dumpling. If it comes out clean, the dumplings are ready; if not, cover again and simmer for a few more minutes.

6. Once the dumplings are cooked, sprinkle with fresh coriander and red onion. Serve with lime wedges for squeezing over.

Pulled Aubergine Steamed Bun

SERVES 2–3

The Chinese word bao means 'bun' and is associated with the fluffy, steamed dumplings that are loved and devoured across China. Their popularity has spread across borders and they are now enjoyed all over the world. They can have an array of fillings from barbecue pork to shiitake and napa cabbage, but here I've used aubergine as it is so versatile and a great sponge for flavour.

FOR THE DUMPLINGS

200g (7oz) plain (all-purpose) flour
2g (scant ½tsp) active dry yeast
1 tsp sugar
100ml (3½fl oz) warm water
1 large or 2 small aubergines (eggplants), finely diced
2 tbsp light soy sauce
1 tsp medium curry powder
1 tsp sugar
½ red chilli, finely chopped
2 garlic cloves, finely chopped or grated
1cm (½in) piece of ginger, grated
1 spring onion (scallion), finely chopped, to garnish

FOR THE DIPPING SAUCE

1 tsp sugar
2 tbsp light soy sauce
½ tbsp rice wine vinegar
½ tbsp chilli oil
1 tsp sesame oil
1 tsp sesame seeds
1 tbsp water

1. Pour the flour into a large bowl and combine the yeast, sugar and warm water in a jug; once it has formed a froth, whisk again and then add to the bowl of flour and stir until combined. Gently knead the dough for a minute until it is soft and bouncy, then cover the bowl in cling film (plastic wrap) or a tea towel and set aside in a warm, dry area for 1–2 hours, or until the dough has doubled in size.

2. Meanwhile, make the filling. Place a frying pan (skillet) over a medium heat and add the diced aubergine, light soy sauce, curry powder, sugar, red chilli, garlic and ginger. Fry for about 5 minutes, stirring frequently. Add 50ml (generous 2½fl oz) water and fry for another 5–10 minutes, or until the aubergine is soft and the water has evaporated. Leave to cool.

3. Once your dough has risen, cut it into 4–6 equal pieces. One by one, flatten the pieces of dough using the ball of your hand and then roll them into round wrappers, about 10cm (4in) in diameter and 7mm (¼in) thick.

4. Place 1 teaspoon of the filling into the centre of each wrapper – don't be tempted to add too much filling as it will be difficult to seal otherwise. Pleat the wrapper in a clockwise motion, pinching it at every turn, until you seal the dumpling wrapper completely. Once the bun is sealed, set aside on a square of parchment paper. Repeat for all the dumplings.

5. Set up a steamer over a high heat. Arrange the buns, still on the parchment paper, in the steamer and cook for 12 minutes – don't remove the lid until your timer goes off. You may need to cook these in batches.

6. Meanwhile, combine all the dipping sauce ingredients in a bowl.

7. Remove the buns from the steamer (they should be puffed up and fluffy) and scatter over the chopped spring onion. Serve with the dipping sauce.

Toasted Lamb Hats in Yoghurt Sauce Topped with Fennel, Orange & Harissa Dressing

SERVES 2

I absolutely love the sweetness of pomegranates, especially when added to savoury dishes. They seem to be a natural partner for anything creamy, nutty or smoky. On the topic of toppings, fennel is often a bit of a 'love it or hate it' ingredient; personally I love its wonderfully mild flavour and crunchy texture. The stars of the dish are the baked lamb dumplings, inspired by a dish from the Levant, shish barak. There are variations of this dish devoured all over Central Asia too, going by the names chuchvara or joshpara. The toasted dumplings are then simmered in a creamy yoghurt sauce to finish off the cooking process and then drizzled with the punchy orange and harissa dressing and topped with crunchy fennel and tangy pomegranate seeds. Phenomenal.

FOR THE DUMPLINGS

200g (7oz) plain (all-purpose) flour, plus extra for dusting
½ tsp sugar
½ tsp salt
1 tsp vegetable oil
1 tbsp olive oil
150g (generous 5oz) lamb mince (ground lamb)
2 tbsp pine nuts, lightly toasted
1 small onion, finely chopped
5g (pinch) roughly chopped parsley
2 garlic cloves, finely chopped or grated
½ tbsp smoked paprika
1 tsp ground cumin
Salt and pepper

FOR THE YOGHURT SAUCE

400g (14oz) natural yoghurt
1 tsp salt
1 tbsp cornflour

1. Begin by making your dough. Tip the flour, sugar, salt and vegetable oil into a large bowl and give it a light mix, then gradually pour in 90ml (3fl oz) water, mixing at the same time. Keep mixing until a shaggy dough forms, then begin kneading with your hand until a rough dough forms. Cover the bowl in cling film (plastic wrap) and set aside while you make the filling.

2. Heat the olive oil in a frying pan (skillet) over a medium heat. Add the lamb mince and fry for 3 minutes until lightly browned, then add the pine nuts, onion, parsley, garlic, paprika and cumin, and season with salt and pepper. Fry for about 8 minutes, stirring frequently, then turn off the heat.

3. Preheat the oven to 200°C/400°F and line a baking tray with parchment paper (or use a non-stick baking tray).

4. Tip the dough out on to a lightly floured work surface and knead for a further minute. Use a rolling pin to roll out the dough until it's 4mm (generous ⅛in) thick. Cut circles out of the dough using a cookie cutter that's 6cm (2in) in diameter. You should be able to cut 16–20 wrappers. Keep the wrappers covered under a damp tea towel to stop them drying out.

CONTINUES OVERLEAF →

CONTINUES
FROM PAGE 100

FOR THE HARISSA DRESSING

1 heaped tbsp rose harissa

1 tbsp lime juice

2 tbsp fresh orange juice

2 tbsp light soy sauce

TO SERVE

Fresh mint, thinly sliced

½ fennel bulb, very thinly sliced,
 including the fronds

Handful of pomegranate seeds

4. One at a time, place a spoonful of the filling into the centre of each wrapper, fold in half and pinch to seal. Then bring the two corners together and pinch to seal. Repeat for all the other dumplings.

5. Place the dumplings on the baking tray and bake in the oven for 10 minutes until lightly browned.

6. Meanwhile, make the yoghurt sauce. Add the yoghurt to a large saucepan (off the heat) and gradually add 200ml (7fl oz) water, a tablespoon at a time, whisking it into the yoghurt each time. After a few spoonfuls, you can gradually add larger amounts of water. This tempers the yoghurt, preventing it from curdling. Once all the water has been added to the yoghurt, stir in the salt and cornflour and then place the pan over a very low heat. Stir until the sauce begins to thicken.

7. Transfer the dumplings from the oven into the pan and cook for a further 10 minutes.

8. Meanwhile, prepare the harissa dressing by combining all the ingredients together in a small bowl. Taste and adjust the seasoning.

9. Spoon the dumplings and creamy sauce into bowls, top with the harissa dressing and finish with fresh mint, sliced fennel slices, fennel fronds and pomegranate seeds.

Pan-Fried Harissa Turkey Dumplings

SERVES 2–3

If you're wondering about the authenticity of this recipe ... well, I made it up. But it's also been one of the most loved dumpling recipes that I've ever shared. Harissa is one of my favourite pantry ingredients. It's a gorgeously hot North African chilli paste that is now enjoyed all over the world. I love this recipe, not only because the flavours work so well together, but also because the dumplings are pretty low maintenance, requiring no pleating skills, just a bit of pinching here and there.

FOR THE DUMPLINGS

200g (7oz) plain (all-purpose) flour, plus extra for dusting
½ tsp salt
200g (7oz) turkey mince (ground turkey)
½ red onion, finely chopped
1 green chilli, thinly sliced
15g (½oz) parsley, finely chopped
2 garlic cloves, finely chopped or grated
1 tsp salt
1 tsp sugar
1 tbsp rose harissa paste
1 tbsp olive oil

TO SERVE

1 tbsp rose harissa paste
4 tbsp Greek yoghurt
Chopped chives

1. Put the flour and salt into a large bowl, give them a stir, then gradually pour in 100ml (3½fl oz) water, mixing at the same time. I use chopsticks to mix my dough but feel free to use a wooden spoon or your hands. Once the mixture resembles a shaggy dough, knead for about a minute until a rough dough has formed. Cover the bowl with cling film (plastic wrap) and set it aside while you make the filling.

2. In a separate large bowl, add all the remaining dumpling ingredients (except the oil) and give them a good mix until everything is well combined.

3. Tip the dough out on to a clean and floured surface. Give it another knead for 1 minute (it should be smoother and more bouncy now). Use a chopstick to spike a hole into the middle of the dough and then continue to stretch it to form a thin-ringed doughnut (with a large hole). Cut the doughnut into about 16–20 equal-sized pieces.

4. Get one piece of dough and press it down with the ball of your hand. Using a rolling pin, roll out the dough into a paper-thin round wrapper, about 1–2mm thick and 8–10cm (3–4in) in diameter. Repeat with all the dough pieces.

CONTINUES OVERLEAF

CONTINUES
FROM PAGE 103

5. Place a spoonful of the filling into the centre of a wrapper, bring the edges of the wrapper up around the filling and pinch at the top to seal. Press it down and then turn it over so that the seam can't be seen. Repeat this step for all dumplings.

6. Place a large frying pan (skillet) over a low heat and drizzle in the olive oil. Add the dumplings to the pan, seam side down, then pour in about 50ml (generous 2½fl oz) boiling water and place a lid on the pan. Steam for 7 minutes, then remove the lid and continue to cook the dumplings until the water has evaporated and the bottom of the dumplings are crispy (you can add a little more oil if necessary). Flip the dumplings and fry for a further 2 minutes so that they're fried on both sides.

7. Meanwhile, combine the rose harissa paste and Greek yoghurt in a bowl.

8. Once your dumplings are cooked, transfer to a plate, top with the harissa yoghurt, scatter with chives and enjoy!

Layered Lamb Dumpling Bake with a Paprika Tomato Drizzle

I love the combination of lamb dumplings with creamy garlicky sauce – topped with the fresh tomato butter with a spike of heat, and I'm in dumpling heaven. Inspired by Bosnian klepe these require no pleating – just fold the wrapper in half over the filling and seal into a triangular shape – so they're a great dish to prepare in advance for a gathering with friends. Just double or triple the quantities depending on how many will be at your table!

FOR THE DUMPLINGS

200g (7oz) plain (all-purpose) flour, plus extra for dusting
½ tsp salt
200g (7oz) lamb mince (ground lamb)
½ white onion, finely chopped
2 garlic cloves, finely chopped or grated
1 tsp dried oregano
1 tsp dried thyme
1 tsp paprika
Salt and pepper

1. Add the flour, salt and 100ml (3½fl oz) water to a large bowl and combine with a spoon, then start kneading in the bowl to form a rough dough. Wrap the ball of dough in cling film (plastic wrap) and leave to rest in the fridge while you make your filling.
2. In a separate bowl, combine the lamb mince, onion, garlic, oregano, thyme and paprika. Season with a big pinch of salt and a teaspoon of pepper.
3. Dust your work surface with flour. Knead your dough for another minute (it should now be smoother and more bouncy) and then use a rolling pin to roll it out into a large rectangle about 2–3mm (⅛in) thick. Using a sharp knife, cut the dough lengthways into strips about 8cm (3in) wide, then cut across the strips to make squares – you should end up with around 20 squares.
4. Place a spoonful of the filling into the centre of each square and fold over to make a triangle, then press the edges firmly, pressing out any air as you seal.
5. Preheat the oven to 210°C/410°F and bring a saucepan of salted water to the boil over a medium-low heat. Reduce the heat to a gentle simmer, add the dumplings and leave to simmer for 3 minutes, stirring often to stop them sticking.

FOR THE CREAMY CHEESY SAUCE

2 tbsp sour cream at room
  temperature
200ml (7fl oz) single (light) cream
1 tbsp grated Parmesan cheese
1 tbsp grated mozzarella cheese

FOR THE TOMATO PAPRIKA BUTTER

1 garlic clove, finely chopped or
  grated
4 cherry tomatoes, finely chopped
1 tsp paprika
2 tbsp butter

6. Meanwhile, make the sauce by combining the sour cream, single cream and grated Parmesan in a bowl. Season with a big pinch of salt and pepper.
7. Carefully drain the cooked dumplings and arrange half of them in a small baking dish. Spoon over half the creamy sauce, then repeat with the remaining dumplings and sauce. Finish by sprinkling over the mozzarella cheese, then bake in the oven for 15 minutes.
8. Meanwhile, make the tomato paprika butter: combine all the ingredients in a small bowl and microwave for 30 seconds (alternatively, melt in a small saucepan over a low heat).
9. When the dumplings are cooked and the cheese is melted and coloured, remove from the oven and drizzle with the tomato paprika butter. Serve and enjoy!

Chicken & Chorizo Bakes with a Chilli Lime Aioli

SERVES 2–3

It is believed that the earliest mention of empanadas is in a 1520s Spanish cookbook; however, some suggest they have been enjoyed around 200–300 years earlier than this! They're a much-loved food, eaten across Latin American countries and I certainly ate my fair share when travelling across South America. One of my fondest memories was in Chile, when we stopped off at the tiny village of Machuca, located at 4,000 metres (13,000 feet) above sea level. We purchased a handful of homemade empanadas from the only little shop in one of the mud huts. They were toasty, comforting and a perfect snack to warm us up at the rather cold temperature of -15°C/5°F. This recipe is inspired by the empanada and filled with a spicy dosage of chicken and chorizo. Oh, and the chilli lime aioli is a must!

FOR THE FILLING

1 tbsp olive oil
½ onion, finely chopped
2 garlic cloves, finely chopped
  or grated
200g (7oz) chicken mince
  (ground chicken)
100g (3½oz) chorizo, finely chopped
1 tsp fresh thyme
1 tsp fresh oregano
1 tsp paprika
100ml (3½fl oz) chicken stock
150g (generous 5oz) peas
Salt and pepper

FOR THE DOUGH

200g plain (all-purpose) flour
90g (3oz) cold unsalted butter, diced
¼ tsp salt
2 medium eggs
Splash of milk

1. First up, make the filling. Heat the oil a large frying pan (skillet) over a medium heat, add the onion and garlic and fry for 3 minutes, stirring frequently, until soft. Add the chicken mince, chorizo, thyme, oregano, paprika and a big pinch of salt and a grind of pepper. Fry for 5 minutes until the chicken is cooked.

2. Pour in the chicken stock and peas and cook for 5 minutes, or until the liquid has evaporated. Remove from the heat and leave to cool.

3. Meanwhile, make your dough. Put the flour in a bowl and add in the diced butter. Rub the butter into the flour using your fingers until the flour becomes crumbly. Stir in salt and one of the eggs and give everything a mix until a shaggy dough forms. Add the milk and mix until you have a soft but not sticky dough. When you start working the dough, it might feel dry, but keep working it and it'll get more malleable. Wrap the dough in cling film (plastic wrap) and chill in the fridge for 30 minutes.

CONTINUES OVERLEAF →

CONTINUES
FROM PAGE 108

FOR THE SAUCE

2 tbsp sour cream

2 tbsp mayonnaise

1 chilli, finely chopped

1 garlic clove, finely chopped or
 grated

1 tbsp lime juice

5g (pinch) chopped fresh coriander
 (cilantro)

4. Turn the dough out on a lightly floured surface and form it into
 a log, then cut the log into 8 equal pieces. Roll each piece out
 into a round wrapper, about 3mm (⅛in) thick and 15cm (6in) in
 diameter.

5. Preheat the oven to 200°C/400°F.

6. Take one of your wrappers and place 2 tablespoons of filling
 on one half of the pastry circle. Spread into a half-moon shape,
 leaving a small border. Fold the wrapper over to form a semicircle
 and crimp the edges with a fork. Repeat for all the other
 wrappers. (If you're looking for a more challenging crimp, fold
 the dumpling in half, seal and then press and twist the dough
 along the edge to form a cute little pattern.)

7. Arrange the filled and sealed dumplings on a baking tray. Lightly
 beat the remaining egg and then brush this over the dumplings.
 Bake in the oven for 20 minutes, or until golden.

8. Meanwhile, combine all the sauce ingredients in a small bowl.
 Taste and season accordingly. Serve alongside the hot baked
 dumplings.

Potato & Ricotta Pockets with Chorizo, Crème Fraîche & Dill

SERVES 2–3

I spent the first four years of my life in Poland and although I was too young to recall eating pierogi, my parents joyfully recount stories of us trotting down to the local corner restaurant and devouring these cheese and potato-filled dumplings. This recipe is a bit of a twist on the traditional – instead of topping the dumplings with bacon, I'm using its spicier cousin, chorizo, to give it a bit of a kick.

FOR THE DUMPLINGS
200g (7oz) plain (all-purpose) flour,
  plus extra for dusting
1 small egg
1 tsp salt
2 potatoes, peeled and cut into
  chunks
1 red onion, finely chopped
100g (3½oz) ricotta cheese
2 garlic cloves, finely chopped
  or grated
Salt and pepper

TO SERVE
1 tbsp butter
75g (2½oz) chorizo, finely chopped
2 tbsp sour cream
3 sprigs of dill, roughly chopped

1. Put the flour, egg, salt and 70ml (2½fl oz) water into a large bowl and stir together with your hand or a wooden spoon until a rough ball begins to form. Transfer the dough to a clean work surface and sprinkle with flour. Knead the dough for a minute – you should be able to do this without it sticking to your hands so if it sticks, add some more flour. Place the ball of dough back into the bowl, cover with cling film (plastic wrap) and set aside for 15 minutes.
2. To make the filling, add the potatoes to a saucepan of salted water and bring to the boil, then leave to simmer for 10 minutes until the potatoes are soft but not falling apart. Drain the potatoes and leave them to cool.
3. Add the cooled potatoes to a bowl and mash until smooth, then add the chopped red onion, ricotta, garlic, a heaped teaspoon of flaky salt and a grind of pepper. Mix together and set aside.
4. Turn the dough out again on to your floured surface and knead for another 30 seconds. It should be smooth and bouncy. Roll the dough out using a rolling pin until your dough is about 2–3mm (⅛in) thick. Use an 8cm (3in) cookie cutter to cut out round wrappers – you should be able to make 16–20 wrappers.
5. Place a teaspoon of filling into the centre of a wrapper, fold it over to make a semicircle and pinch the edges to seal. Repeat this step for all the wrappers and filling.

CONTINUES
OVERLEAF

6. Bring a large saucepan of salted water to the boil. Gently lower your dumplings into the pan, reduce the heat and leave to simmer for 5 minutes, then drain carefully.

7. While the dumplings are simmering, melt the butter in a frying pan (skillet) over a high heat. Add the diced chorizo and fry for a minute or two, then remove from the pan. Add the drained dumplings to the frying pan and fry for 3 minutes on each side, or until they begin to show some colour all over.

8. Spoon the sour cream on to your serving plate and spread it out. Top with the dumplings, fried chorizo and dill. Enjoy!

Dumpling Wreath

This makes a seriously impressive centrepiece, especially when you consider how easy it is to make. Oroma (orama) is a traditional spiralled dumpling that can be found in countries across Central Asia, including Kazakhstan, Kyrgyzstan, Uzbekistan and Mongolia. My non-traditional version includes a spiced beef and grated carrot filling with several garnishes to add heat and vibrancy, including yoghurt, harissa paste, chives, coriander and sliced chilli.

FOR THE DOUGH
200g (7oz) plain (all-purpose) flour, plus extra for dusting
1 tsp salt

FOR THE FILLING
200g (7oz) 20% fat beef mince (ground beef)
1 carrot, grated
1 tsp flaky salt
2 tsp dried mixed herbs
1 tsp smoked paprika
1 tsp ground cumin
½ red onion, finely diced
Olive oil, for brushing the dough

TO SERVE
5 tbsp Greek yoghurt
1 tbsp harissa paste mixed with 2 tbsp olive oil
Hanfdul of chives, finely chopped
Bunch of coriander (cilantro), finely chopped
1 large red chilli, thinly sliced

1. Begin by making your dough. Add the flour and salt to a large bowl and gradually pour in 100ml (3½fl oz) water, while at the same time stirring with chopsticks or a wooden spoon. Combine until a shaggy dough forms, then begin kneading with your hand for 1 minute until you have a rough dough. You don't want the dough to stick to your hands; if it does once you've kneaded it, add more flour to dry it out. Wrap the ball of dough in cling film (plastic wrap) and set it aside.

2. Put the beef mince, grated carrot, salt, mixed herbs, smoked paprika and ground cumin in a large bowl and give everything a good mix, then set aside.

3. Turn the dough out on a floured surface and knead it for another 30 seconds, then roll it out using a rolling pin into a large, very thin rectangle of dough, about 25 x 30cm (10–12in) and 1–2mm thick (paper thin).

4. Brush the dough with olive oil, evenly spread the beef mince mixture all over the surface, then scatter over the chopped red onion. Starting at one of the long ends, gently roll the dough into a long log. Don't worry if the dough tears.

5. Prepare a steamer. Cut a circle of parchment paper that will fit inside your steaming basket and cut out little breathing holes. Place it inside the steaming basket and add the dumpling roll: get both ends of the roll and pinch them together to form a circular wreath. Steam for 12 minutes.

6. Once your dumpling wreath is cooked, remove it gently from the steamer and transfer to a serving plate. Top with the yoghurt, harissa oil, chives, coriander and chilli. Enjoy!

Gochujang 'Potato-Pillow' Lasagne

SERVES 4

We're landing somewhere in between Korea and Italy for this recipe. The simple homemade potato gnocchi acts as your deconstructed pasta, which is then married with a fiery gochujang ragu and creamy bechamel sauce. Honestly, the flavours are phenomenal, and it's one of my favourite dishes to make when I've got friends coming over. It's a medley of ingredients that people often haven't experienced before but trust me when I say it never fails to impress. If you're looking for a lighter or speedier option, replacing the gnocchi with big fat juicy butter beans works equally well.

FOR THE DUMPLINGS

400g (14oz) floury potatoes, such as Ukon or Maris Piper
1 egg yolk
¼ tsp fine sea salt
100g (3½oz) '00' flour, plus extra as needed
Semolina or cornflour, for dusting

FOR THE GOCHUJANG RAGU

2 tbsp olive oil
1 red onion, finely diced
2 garlic cloves, finely chopped or grated
2 spring onions (scallions), thinly sliced
400g (14oz) 20% fat beef mince (ground beef)
1 tsp paprika
1 tsp sugar
2 tbsp gochujang
1 tbsp tomato purée
400g (14oz) tin tomatoes
400ml (13½fl oz) chicken/beef/veg stock
Salt and pepper

1. Boil the potatoes in their skins for about 20 minutes, or until you can pierce them easily with a fork. Drain and set aside to cool slightly. Once they are cool enough to handle, peel off the skins and then pass through a potato ricer over a large bowl. If you don't have a potato ricer, use a potato masher to thoroughly mash the potato until there are little to no lumps.

2. Add the egg yolk and salt to the potatoes, along with a few tablespoons of the flour. Gently mix a few times with a fork to combine, gradually adding the rest of the flour as you go (only add more flour if the dough keeps sticking to the fork). Once the dough starts to come together, use your hands to bring it together to form a ball. If it feels too wet, then add more flour – it should feel like a light play dough. Once you have a soft dough, cover the bowl with cling film (plastic wrap) and set aside while you make your ragu.

3. Heat the olive oil in a large casserole dish over a medium heat. Add the onion, garlic and spring onions and fry for 5 minutes, or until the onions become soft. Add the beef mince and fry for a further 5 minutes, then add the remaining ingredients. Give everything a good stir and simmer over a low heat for a further 10 minutes. Season to taste with salt and pepper.

CONTINUES OVERLEAF

FOR THE BECHAMEL SAUCE AND TOPPING

4 tbsp salted butter

4 tbsp plain flour

500ml (generous 1 pint) milk

80g (3oz) Cheddar cheese, grated

3 tbsp grated Parmesan cheese

¼ tsp grated nutmeg

125g (4½oz) mozzarella cheese, torn into chunks

4. While that's simmering away, cut the dough ball into 4 equal pieces. Roll one piece into a log about 15cm (6in) long, then cut the log into 10–15 pieces, about 1cm (½in) in size, to create little pillows of gnocchi. Using the back of a fork, roll your gnocchi down the tines, giving them the classic gnocchi lines. Transfer to a plate dusted with semolina or cornflour to prevent them sticking, then repeat with the remaining pieces of dough. If you're short on time, you can skip the fork rolling step and just add them in as little pillows of joy.

5. To make the bechamel sauce, melt the butter in a saucepan over a medium heat. Add the flour and whisk together until the flour and butter combine. Cook for a couple of minutes, then gradually pour in the milk, whisking continuously until you have a thick white sauce. Keep whisking to avoid any lumps. Add half the grated Cheddar, all the Parmesan and the nutmeg, then season to taste with salt and pepper.

6. Preheat the oven to 200°C/400°F.

7. Add the gnocchi to your beef ragu dish and gently stir so the gnocchi are evenly coated and spread throughout the dish. Pour the bechamel sauce evenly over the top of the ragu, then sprinkle it with the remaining Cheddar and the chunks of mozzarella. Bake in the oven for 20 minutes until bubbling and hot on top.

Open-top Tofu & Mushroom Baskets with Tahini Chilli Noodles

SERVES 2–3

Chinese siu mai is a popular style of dim sum with an open top, commonly filled with pork and prawn. This cute tofu and mushroom number is my plant-based version. I've chosen to serve them with spicy noodles, but they're just as delicious eaten on their own, with a bit of chilli oil.

FOR THE DUMPLINGS
100g (3½oz) firm tofu
85g (3oz) mushrooms
2 spring onions (scallions)
2 garlic cloves
1cm (½in) piece of ginger
1 tsp sugar
2 tbsp cornflour (cornstarch)
1 tbsp light soy sauce
½ tbsp sesame oil
½ tbsp rice wine vinegar
12–15 round dumpling wrappers
  (ensure they are vegan)
½ carrot, finely diced
Salt and black pepper

FOR THE NOODLES
2 nests of wheat noodles
2 tbsp tahini
1 tbsp peanut butter
2 tbsp light soy sauce
½ tbsp balsamic vinegar
1 tsp sugar
2 tbsp chilli oil
1 tbsp vegan hoisin sauce
½ tsp Chinese five-spice (optional)
150ml (5fl oz) boiling vegetable stock
1 spring onion (scallion), finely
  chopped

1. Add the tofu, mushrooms, spring onions, garlic cloves, ginger, sugar, cornflour, light soy sauce, sesame oil, rice wine vinegar and a pinch of salt and pepper to a food processor and blitz until a relatively thick, smooth paste has formed. Transfer to a bowl.

2. Get your wrappers but keep them under a damp tea towel so they don't dry out. One by one, place a dumpling wrapper on a clean surface and lightly wet the edges, then add a heaped teaspoon of the filling to the centre of the wrapper. Make a circle with your thumb and index finger on your left hand (assuming you are right-handed, otherwise use your right hand). Balance the dumpling wrapper and filling over the hole in your hand then gently ease the whole thing downwards through the hole. This will wrap the dough around the filling leaving the top exposed. Firmly but gently press the wrapper together until it keeps its shape so that it looks like a little tub full of tofu and mushroom filling. Set aside and repeat for the rest of the dumplings.

3. If you're using a metal steamer basket, I'd recommend brushing it with oil so the dumplings don't stick. Place the dumplings in your steamer and then sprinkle little pinches of the diced carrot on top of each dumpling. Cook for 6–7 minutes.

4. While the dumplings are cooking, cook the noodles according to the packet instructions.

5. Combine the tahini, peanut butter, light soy sauce, balsamic vinegar, sugar, chilli oil, vegan hoisin sauce and Chinese five-spice in a bowl and whisk vigorously. Taste and adjust the seasoning, then divide this between 2–3 serving bowls.

6. Evenly pour the hot stock into the bowls and mix well. Add the noodles and top with the cooked dumplings and chopped spring onion.

Feta, Mint & Spinach Pockets

SERVES 2–3

Eating these feta, mint and spinach parcels always reminds me of being on holiday in Greece. One morning, while visiting Hydra – a small island off the coast of the mainland – we woke up for the sunrise. It's my favourite time of day because everyone is asleep apart from the local bakers setting up their shops and the farmers trotting around on donkeys, clip-clopping on the cobbled streets. After enjoying the sunrise, we toddled down to the cute bakery on the main street and bought several Greek pastries including spanakopita – a savoury feta and spinach pie. Sitting on the sea front, we'd gobble up our pastries and feel like life really couldn't be better. These spanakopita-inspired baked parcels are a homage to Greece and their glorious pastries.

100g (3½oz) spinach
200g (7oz) feta cheese
35g (generous 1oz) grated Parmesan cheese
2 garlic cloves, finely chopped or grated
1 small white onion, finely chopped
3 eggs
1 tbsp finely chopped mint
270g (9½oz) filo pastry, or 8 sheets
Melted butter, for brushing
1 tbsp sesame seeds
1 tbsp honey
Black pepper

1. Preheat the oven to 200°C/400°F.
2. Place the spinach in a colander and pour over boiling water from the kettle until it's wilted, then rinse with cold water. Allow to drain, then squeeze any excess water out of the spinach and roughly chop.
3. Add the chopped spinach to a large bowl along with the feta, Parmesan, garlic, onion, two of the eggs, chopped mint and a grind of black pepper. Give everything a good mix until well combined.
4. Get your sheets of filo out but keep them covered under a damp tea towel to stop them drying out. Lay a filo sheet down and lightly brush with melted butter, then fold the filo sheet vertically into three, so you have a long strip. Add 1 heaped tablespoon of the filling to the base of the strip and then fold the bottom corner up and over to make a triangle shape. Keep folding over, working your way to the top of the pastry strip, maintaining the triangle shape as you go. Repeat this step to make all 8 pockets, placing them on a baking tray as you finish each one.
5. Lightly beat the remaining egg and then brush this over the pastry parcels. Sprinkle with sesame seeds and bake in the oven for 25 minutes, or until golden and crispy.
6. Remove from the oven, drizzle with honey and serve!

Chicken & Lemongrass Pockets in a Fiery Fish Noodle Soup

SERVES 2

Lemongrass is a staple ingredient in Vietnamese cuisine with a citrus-like flavour that transforms the most simple, basic dishes into something really special. In addition to the juicy, aromatic chicken and lemongrass dumplings, this straightforward broth recipe requires minimal effort, but you're rewarded with oodles of flavour.

FOR THE DUMPLINGS

200g (7oz) chicken mince (ground chicken)
1 lemongrass stick, top and tailed, bashed and finely chopped
1cm (½in) piece of ginger, grated
2 garlic cloves, finely chopped or grated
1 tbsp fish sauce
1 red chilli, finely chopped
1 tsp sugar
15g (½oz) finely chopped coriander (cilantro)
16–20 square dumpling wrappers

FOR THE NOODLES

1 litre (2 pints) hot fish stock
1 tbsp light soy sauce
1 tbsp fish sauce
1 tbsp sugar
½ tbsp rice wine vinegar
1 tbsp chilli oil
200g (7oz) udon noodles

TO SERVE

2–3 lime wedges
Bunch of coriander
50g (scant 2oz) edamame beans
1 large red chilli, thinly sliced
1 carrot, peeled into thin strips

1. Begin by combining all the dumpling ingredients (except the wrappers) in a bowl until you have a rough paste.
2. Get your dumpling wrappers out but keep them under a damp tea towel to prevent them drying out.
3. Working on one at a time, place a heaped teaspoon of the filling into the centre of the wrapper, lightly wet the edges of the wrapper with your finger and then fold the wrapper in half to make a triangle and seal the edges. Bring two opposite triangle edges together and pinch to seal. Repeat with the remaining wrappers and filling.
4. Pour the hot fish stock into a large saucepan followed by the light soy sauce, fish sauce, sugar, rice wine vinegar and chilli oil and place over a low heat. Carefully add the dumplings and simmer for 4 minutes, then add the udon noodles and cook for a further 2 minutes. Taste the broth and season with more soy sauce, fish sauce or sugar, as needed.
5. Divide the dumplings, noodles and broth between 2 bowls and top with lime wedges, coriander, edamame beans, carrot and chilli.

Stuffed Potato Boulders with Stir-fried Sausage, Apple & Cabbage

SERVES 4

This simple dish is far greater than the sum of its parts: potato, cheese, sausage, apple and cabbage. Make it, and you'll find yourself in comfort heaven. Kartoffelklösse are a type of potato dumpling known throughout Germany, Switzerland and Austria. They're often filled with croutons, meats or sauerkraut, but for this version I've stuffed them with cheese. The cheesy potato dumplings are then placed on a bed of stir-fried sausage, apple and cabbage. Gently spiced, with a slight crunch, and astonishingly tasty (given how easy it is), this recipe is a go-to of mine when looking for a wholesome dish during the winter months.

FOR THE DUMPLINGS
400g (14oz) floury potatoes (Yukon or Maris Piper), peeled and roughly chopped
⅛ tsp grated nutmeg
¼ tsp paprika
1 large egg
50g (scant 2oz) plain (all-purpose) flour
100g (3½oz) buffalo mozzarella cheese, cut into 4 cubes
1 tbsp olive oil
Salt and pepper

FOR THE CABBAGE & SAUSAGES
Drizzle of olive oil
300g (10½oz) sausages
300g (10½oz) red cabbage, very thinly sliced
1 apple, peeled and finely chopped
1 tbsp sugar
1 tbsp balsamic vinegar
Chopped chives, to garnish

1. Place the potatoes in a large saucepan of salted water and bring to the boil. Reduce the heat to medium-low and simmer for 10–15 minutes, or until you can pierce the potatoes easily with a fork. Drain and allow to cool a little.

2. Tip the cooled potatoes into a large bowl and mash with the nutmeg, paprika, a teaspoon of salt and some pepper using a fork or potato masher (or put through a potato ricer). Add the egg and mash until combined, then sprinkle in the flour and mix gently with your hand or a spoon. Don't overmix as this will cause the dumplings to become dense. If the mixture is sticky, add more flour.

3. Preheat the oven to 190°C/375°F.

4. Scoop a quarter of the dough into the palm of your hand and shape the dough into a circle. Place a cube of mozzarella in the centre of the circle, then pull the dough around the mozzarella and seal it. Roll into a smooth ball, then repeat to make 4 dumplings in total.

CONTINUES OVERLEAF

CONTINUES
FROM PAGE 124

5. Drizzle the oil into an ovenproof dish and pour in about
    2 tablespoons of water. Arrange the dumplings in the dish,
    cover with foil and bake in the oven for 15 minutes. Remove
    the foil and bake for a further 10 minutes.
6. Meanwhile, place a frying pan (skillet) over a high heat and
    drizzle with oil. Squeeze the sausage meat out of the casings
    and then add to the pan, breaking it up with a spatula or
    wooden spoon. Once the sausage meat is crumbly in texture
    and starting to colour, reduce the heat to medium and add
    the red cabbage, apple and 100ml (3½fl oz) water. Add a big
    pinch of flaky salt and a grind of pepper. Stir frequently for
    10 minutes until the water has evaporated, then reduce the
    heat to low and sprinkle over the sugar and balsamic vinegar.
    Taste and adjust the seasoning.
7. Once the cabbage and sausage mixture is tender and your
    dumplings are ready, divide the mixture between 4 plates and
    top with your dumplings. Sprinkle with chives and enjoy!

Egg Envelopes with a Ginger Pork Filling

SERVES 2–3

Chinese dan jiao (egg dumplings) are absolutely delicious - a light, juicy, savoury meat filling is enveloped in an egg omelette wrapper, then gently simmered in chicken broth and served with spring onion and chilli. Make sure to use a super non-stick pan for these, otherwise your dumplings might become a deconstructed omelette (we don't want that now, do we).

FOR THE FILLING

1 spring onion (scallion), finely chopped
1 garlic clove, finely chopped or grated
1cm (½in) piece of ginger, grated
200g (7oz) pork mince (ground pork)
1 tbsp gluten-free light soy sauce
½ tbsp sesame oil
½ tbsp rice wine vinegar
½ tsp ground black pepper
½ tsp chilli flakes

FOR THE GLUTEN-FREE EGG WRAPPERS

8 eggs, beaten
2 tbsp potato, tapioca starch
  or cornflour (cornstarch)
Drizzle of vegetable oil

FOR THE SAUCE

500ml (generous 1 pint) hot chicken
  stock
1 tsp gluten-free light soy sauce
1 tsp sesame oil
½ tsp rice wine vinegar
1 tsp cornflour (cornstarch)

TO SERVE

1 spring onion (scallion), finely
  chopped
½ red chilli, finely chopped
1 tsp black sesame seeds

1. Combine all the filling ingredients together in a bowl using a chopstick or fork until you have a rough paste-like consistency. Set aside while you make the egg wrappers.

2. Add the eggs, starch or cornflour and 4 tablespoons water to a jug and mix together until well combined.

3. Place a large non-stick frying pan (skillet) over a medium-low heat and drizzle with some vegetable oil. Once your pan is hot, pour a large spoonful (2–3 tablespoons) of the egg mixture into your pan and form it into a rough circle about 10cm (4in) in diameter, using a spatula. When the underside is slightly cooked, after 20 seconds, and the top is still moist, transfer to a clean work surface and add a teaspoon of the filling into the centre of the wrapper. Gently fold over the wrapper using a spatula and a spoon (or your fingers if they're asbestos), into a semicircle and seal gently. Set aside and repeat this step until the egg mixture and filling are used up. You should be able to make about 16 dumplings.

4. Pour the hot chicken stock into the same frying pan, along with the light soy sauce, sesame oil, rice wine vinegar and cornflour. Place over a low heat, then gently add the sealed egg dumplings. Cover with a lid and simmer for 4 minutes with the lid on, then another 4 minutes with the lid off.

5. Remove the dumplings and gently transfer to serving plates. Drizzle over the chicken stock sauce and scatter with chopped spring onion, chilli and sesame seeds.

French Onion Dumpling Soup

SERVES 2–3

School lunches often get a bad rep, but for me growing up in rural France, they meant something quite different. School lunches were taken seriously there, and they were the highlight of my day. Every day we were treated to a three-course meal; Olivier, the school chef, would wheel out his trolley, serving up generous platters of freshly-made food to each table. We eagerly divided and devoured each dish. One of my all-time favourites was the classic French onion soup and here I've added a twist to the recipe by including the delightful German dumplings known as spaetzle: tiny, noodle-like egg dumplings that are a breeze to prepare and cook in minutes. They complement the French onion soup perfectly, adding an extra dimension of texture, bite and heartiness. Of course, there's no harm in dipping a bit of bread too, but trust me, with these dumplings, you won't need it. Bon appétit!

FOR THE DUMPLINGS
250g (9oz) plain (all-purpose) flour
2 eggs
200ml (7fl oz) milk
½ tsp fine salt

FOR THE SOUP
25g (scant 1 oz) butter
1 tbsp olive oil
3 large onions, halved and thinly sliced
1 tsp sugar
1 tsp balsamic vinegar
2 garlic cloves
1 tbsp plain flour
100ml (3½fl oz) dry white wine
1 litre (2 pints) beef stock
Salt and pepper

TO SERVE
50g (scant 2oz) grated Gruyère cheese
Chopped chives

1. First up, make the dumplings. Add the flour, eggs, milk and salt to a large bowl and whisk until you have a thick pancake batter. Set aside in the fridge while you make your soup.

2. Heat the butter and oil in a large saucepan over a medium heat; once the butter has melted add the onions and season with salt and pepper. Fry for 20 minutes, stirring frequently, then add the sugar, balsamic vinegar and garlic and fry for another 5 minutes.

3. Stir in the flour and cook for a minute or two, then pour in the wine, stirring to combine. Let the wine evaporate a bit, then add the beef stock. Bring to the boil, then reduce the heat and leave to simmer for 10 minutes. Taste and adjust the seasoning.

4. Get your dumpling batter from the fridge. Place a flat colander or something with small holes over the soup and pour half the dough mixture into it. Using a spatula, push the dough through the colander, letting it drop into the soup. Repeat with the second half of the batter.

5. Once you've run out of dough, give the soup a stir and leave the dumplings to cook for another minute, or until they have all risen to the top.

6. Ladle the soup into bowls and serve scattered with grated Gruyère and chives.

Mini Jerk Chicken Fried Dumpling Burgers

SERVES 2

Marinating is all about building flavour. And the longer you marinate your chicken for, the better the flavour and the juicier and more tender the meat is. This recipe is a twist on the classic Jamaican dumplings – fried dumplings, traditionally eaten for breakfast or lunch, paired with ackee and saltfish, stew or scrambled eggs, to name a few. My twist involves frying the dumplings as normal, but then slicing them in half and filling them with fried jerk chicken and salsa. The flavours pop and work unbelievably well together. It's also just a fun and more unique way to serve dumplings! The jerk marinade may have a lengthy ingredients list but trust me when I say the result is pretty awesome. Fiery, aromatic and fresh, these will be the best dumpling burgers you'll ever make.

FOR THE MARINATED CHICKEN

1 scotch bonnet chilli
50ml (generous 2½fl oz) light soy sauce
2 tbsp olive oil, plus extra for frying
2 tbsp Worcestershire sauce
2 tbsp white wine vinegar
1 tbsp brown sugar
1 tsp ground cinnamon
1 tbsp ground allspice
1 tbsp dried thyme
1 tsp grated nutmeg
2 spring onions (scallions), chopped
2.5cm (1in) piece of ginger
1 shallot, halved
3 garlic cloves
Juice of 1 lime
4 skinless chicken thigh fillets
Salt and pepper

FOR THE BURGER SALSA

½ mango, finely chopped into cubes
½ red (bell) pepper, finely chopped
½ red onion, thinly sliced
1 avocado, finely chopped
Juice of 1 lime
1 tbsp olive oil

1. Start by marinating the chicken. Add the scotch bonnet chilli, light soy sauce, olive oil, Worcestershire sauce, white wine vinegar, brown sugar, cinnamon, allspice, dried thyme, nutmeg, spring onions, ginger, shallot, garlic, lime juice and a pinch of salt and pepper to a blender and blitz until smooth.

2. Put the chicken thighs into a bowl, pour over most of the marinade (set aside 2 tablespoons in a bowl for later) and mix together. Cover with cling film (plastic wrap) and set aside in the fridge for at least 20 minutes (if you can leave them overnight in the fridge, the flavours will be unreal).

3. Next up, make your burger salsa by combining all the ingredients in a bowl. Season to taste with salt and pepper.

4. To make the dumplings, combine the self-raising flour, baking powder, salt and sugar in a large bowl. Give it a mix and then gradually pour in 100ml (3fl oz) water, mixing with your hands or a wooden spoon until the dough has combined. Don't knead as this will cause the dumplings to become dense.

CONTINUES OVERLEAF →

CONTINUES
FROM PAGE 126

FOR THE DUMPLINGS

200g (generous 5oz) self-raising
  (self-rising) flour
2 tsp baking powder
½ tsp fine salt
1 tsp sugar
Vegetable oil, for frying

TO SERVE

3 tbsp mayonnaise
Cheese slices

5. Pour enough oil into a heavy-based saucepan so that it's around 10cm (4in) deep and place it over a medium heat. Meanwhile, divide the dough into 8 pieces and shape them into little patties, around 1.5cm (¾in) thick and 7cm (2½in) wide. Check that the oil is hot enough by putting the handle of a wooden spoon in the oil; if bubbles form around it then the oil is ready. Use a slotted spoon to carefully lower the dumplings into the oil and fry until golden brown, around 3–4 minutes on each side (you may need to fry these in batches). When they are puffed up and golden remove from the pan and drain on a plate lined with kitchen paper (kitchen towel).

6. To cook the chicken, heat a splash of olive oil in a frying pan (skillet) over a medium heat, add the marinated chicken thighs and fry for 4 minutes on each side. Remove, set aside, and slice each one in half.

7. Combine the 2 tablespoons of reserved marinade with the mayonnaise. Taste and add more mayonnaise if needed.

8. Meanwhile, split your dumplings in half. Add a dollop of the jerk mayonnaise to the base of the bun, then top with half a chicken thigh, a piece of cheese and some burger salsa. Serve up and enjoy!

Spinach & Artichoke Balls in a Butter Cream & Sage Sauce

SERVES 2–3

Growing up in the Czech Republic for six years meant that I was fortunate enough to learn how to ski. Many years later I went skiing in Austria where they have the most delicious spinach bread dumplings called spinatknödel. They're easy to make and are a really great dumpling for when you're in need of warming up. My variation includes artichoke – simply because I love it.

FOR THE DUMPLINGS

200g (7oz) bread (preferably stale), cut into small cubes

75ml (2½fl oz) milk

2 eggs, beaten

50g (scant 2oz) grated vegetarian Parmesan cheese, plus extra to serve

200g (7oz) frozen spinach, thawed and excess water squeezed out

100g (3½oz) tinned artichokes, drained and finely chopped

2 garlic cloves, finely chopped or grated

Flour, for dusting

FOR THE SAUCE

50g (scant 2oz) butter

10 sage leaves or 1 tbsp dried sage

150ml (5fl oz) cream

Salt and pepper

1. Add the bread cubes to a large bowl and pour over the milk and beaten eggs. Season with salt and pepper and leave to soak for 5 minutes.

2. Add the remaining dumpling ingredients to a food processor with the soaked bread cube mixture. Blend until a roughly chopped paste has formed. Pour back into your large bowl. You want the ingredients to form into a ball without being too sticky, so add flour until the mixture stops sticking to your hands. Don't knead as this will make them dense. Once a rough dough has formed, cover the bowl in cling film (plastic wrap) and set aside to rest for 15 minutes.

3. Gently wet your hands and divide the dough into 8 equal-sized portions and roll into balls. Toss the balls in a bowl of flour to seal them and then set aside ready to be cooked.

4. Once you've rolled your dumpling balls, place them in a pan of salted boiling water on low heat and gently lower the dumplings into the saucepan. Simmer for 10–15 minutes until the dumplings float and bob on the surface.

5. Meanwhile, place a frying pan on medium-low heat. Add the in butter and once melted, add in the sage. Once the butter is foaming, add in your cream, salt and pepper. Give it a mix, then divide the sauce between your plates.

6. Once your dumplings are cooked, remove from the pan using a slotted spoon and arrange them on top of the sage cream butter. Top with grated Parmesan.

SERVES 2-3

Pork & Vermicelli Cabbage Rolls

While vegetables like okra, aubergine and pak choi have found their way into my culinary repertoire over the past decade, cabbage has been a firm staple in my kitchen for as long as I can remember. Over the years, however, my approach to preparing and enjoying it has evolved from the boiled, slightly overcooked style to creations like these delectable cabbage roll dumplings. I could honestly indulge in them all day until I'm ready to burst. Packed with flavour and offering a delightful array of textures, they're a sensory delight. Cabbage rolls, in their diverse forms, can be found across Europe as well as in China. For this particular recipe, I've drawn inspiration from Vietnamese cuisine, incorporating vibrant flavours such as mint, coriander and fish sauce, harmoniously paired with pork mince, vermicelli noodles, bird's eye chillies and carrot. The slightly addictive dipping sauce will leave you craving for more with each bite.

FOR THE CABBAGE ROLL DUMPLINGS

12 savoy or napa cabbage leaves
50g (scant 2oz) vermicelli noodles
2 garlic cloves, finely chopped or grated
1 bird's eye green chilli, thinly sliced
1 carrot, grated
5g (pinch) sliced coriander (cilantro) leaves
5g (pinch) sliced mint leaves
250g (9oz) 20% fat pork mince (ground pork)
1 tbsp sugar
2 tbsp fish sauce
2 tbsp rice wine vinegar
1 tbsp cornflour (cornstarch)
½ tsp black pepper

FOR THE DIPPING SAUCE

1 tbsp fish sauce
1 tbsp sugar
1 tbsp rice wine vinegar
1 green bird's eye chilli, finely chopped
Juice of ½ lime
4 tbsp boiling water

1. Blanch the cabbage leaves in a large saucepan of boiling water for a couple of minutes, then drain and refresh in cold water. Place them on a chopping board and trim out any thick stems.

2. Cook the vermicelli noodles according to the packet instructions, then drain and chop them loosely with scissors.

3. Combine all the remaining dumpling ingredients in a large bowl. Add the snipped noodles and mix well until everything is thoroughly combined.

4. Place a cabbage leaf down with the removed stem side closest to you on a clean surface or chopping board. Place a large spoonful of the filling at the bottom (stem end) of the leaf, then tuck and fold the leaf into a little roll. Repeat this for all the cabbage rolls.

5. Place your cabbage dumplings into a steamer and cook for about 10–12 minutes.

6. Meanwhile, combine all the dipping sauce ingredients in a small bowl, stirring until the sugar has dissolved. Taste and adjust the seasoning.

7. Once your cabbage dumplings are cooked, serve them up with your dipping sauce.

Sesame Crisp Squash & Turkey Dumplings in Ginger Broth

In China, the versatility of wontons extends beyond their delicious fillings to the intricate shapes they can be folded into. During our travels, these tasty parcels became a much-loved part of our adventure, none more so than when enjoyed in a steaming bowl of noodle soup. Believe it or not, hot wonton noodle soup was one of my favourite ways to start the day, especially on travel days. While waiting for any high-speed train, I'd sit down at a bustling pop-up restaurant at the station and enjoy a bowl of the stuff. It was a glorious way to pass the time, and a warming feeling I'll always remember. For this recipe, I've decided to keep things pretty

FOR THE DUMPLINGS

250g (9oz) butternut squash, peeled and cut into small cubes
1 tsp chilli powder
Vegetable oil, for drizzling
200g (7oz) turkey mince (ground turkey)
2 tbsp light soy sauce
1 tbsp honey
2 spring onions (scallions), finely chopped
1 garlic clove, finely chopped or grated
1cm (½in) piece of ginger, grated
16–20 square or round dumpling wrappers
3 tbsp sesame seeds
Salt and pepper

1. Preheat the oven to 180°C/350°F.
2. Place your butternut squash on a baking tray. Sprinkle over the chilli powder and season with salt and pepper. Drizzle with vegetable oil, cover with foil and bake in the oven for 20–30 minutes, or until soft.
3. Transfer the cooked butternut squash to a bowl with the turkey mince, light soy sauce, honey, chopped spring onions, garlic and ginger. Combine everything but don't break down the butternut squash cubes – you want to keep them whole so you get a nice bite in the dumplings. Season with salt and pepper.
4. Get your dumpling wrappers out but keep them under a damp tea towel so that they don't dry out.
5. One at a time, take a wrapper and place a heaped teaspoon of the filling into the centre. Bring all four corners up together in the centre and pinch. Then seal down each of the four sides of the dumpling to make a kite-like shape. Repeat with the rest of the wrappers and filling.
6. Pour the sesame seeds into a bowl and fill another bowl with water. Lightly dunk the base of each dumpling into the water and then into the bowl of sesame seeds so that the base is coated.

simple, and fold them into kite-like designs (not very traditional). The reason for doing this is because it gives them a large surface area on the bottom, perfect for dabbing into sesame seeds to create a crispy underside, which complements the turkey squash filling and aromatic ginger chilli broth. This bowl of goodness is especially delicious when you're feeling a bit under the weather, but I just love eating it any day regardless of how I'm feeling.

FOR THE BROTH

2 tbsp olive oil
1cm (½in) piece of ginger, grated
2 garlic cloves, finely chopped
 or grated
1 red chilli, finely chopped
600ml (20fl oz) chicken or veg stock
2 tbsp light soy sauce
2 tbsp rice wine vinegar
1 tsp sugar

TO GARNISH

Chopped spring onions (scallions)
Chilli oil
Sesame seeds

7. Place a non-stick frying pan (skillet) over a medium heat and drizzle with oil. Add the dumplings and fry for 2 minutes, then reduce the heat, add 50ml (scant 2fl oz) water and cover with a lid. Steam for 6 minutes, then remove the lid and fry until the bottoms of the dumplings are crispy.

8. Meanwhile, make your broth. Heat the olive oil in a saucepan over a medium heat, then add the ginger, garlic and chilli. Fry for 30 seconds, then add chicken stock, light soy sauce, rice wine vinegar and sugar. Stir and bring to the boil, then leave to simmer over a low heat for 10 minutes. Taste and adjust the seasoning.

9. Transfer the dumplings to your serving bowls and ladle in your broth. Top with spring onions, chilli oil and sesame seeds.

Brothy Spinach & Beef Parcels

SERVES 2–3

These soupy spinach and beef parcels are inspired by the traditional Schwäbische Maultaschen, a dish so good that in 2009 the European Union took measures to protect the integrity of the dish by mandating that genuine Maultaschen can only be produced in Swabia – a historical region in Germany – due to its significant cultural importance. So, although these are not genuine Maultaschen, they are a fitting tribute to the real thing.

FOR THE DUMPLINGS

200g (7oz) plain (all-purpose) flour, plus extra for dusting
2 eggs
1 tbsp olive oil
1 onion, finely chopped
15g (½oz) roughly chopped parsley
100g (3½oz) frozen spinach, defrosted and roughly chopped
200g (7oz) beef mince (ground beef)
100g (3½oz) cream cheese
¼ tsp grated nutmeg
Salt and pepper

FOR THE STOCK AND GARNISHES

1 litre (2 pints) hot beef stock
2–3 tsp sour cream
Handful of chives, chopped

1. To make the dough, add the flour to a bowl and create a little well in the centre. Add the eggs, ½ tablespoon of the olive oil and ¼ teaspoon salt and mix with a wooden spoon or your hands. Once the dough has come together, knead for 3–5 minutes, or until you have a soft and bouncy dough. Wrap the dough in cling film (plastic wrap) and put it in the fridge while you make your filling.

2. Put the chopped onion, parsley, spinach, beef mince, cream cheese and nutmeg in a bowl and season with salt and pepper. Give it a good mix until a smooth paste has formed.

3. Get your dough out and place it on a floured work surface. Cut the dough in half and roll it through a pasta machine. Dust liberally with flour and keep rolling until the dough is around 1–2mm thick (paper thin). If you don't have a pasta machine, use a rolling pin. Repeat with the second piece of dough, then cut the pasta sheets into 8 x 10cm (3 x 4in) wrappers.

4. Add a large spoonful of the pork mixture to the centre of each wrapper and spread it out slightly, leaving a 1cm (½in) border. Fold over a third of the square up into the middle of the parcel and then continue to fold over the dumpling to form a sealed parcel (almost like a letter that you're folding into three to fit it into an envelope). Gently pinch the edges to seal. Repeat this step for all dumplings.

5. Pour the hot stock into a saucepan and place over a medium heat. Carefully add the dumplings, then reduce the heat to low and simmer the dumplings for 8 minutes. Remove with a slotted spoon and transfer to your serving bowls.

6. Ladle the beef stock into the bowls, then top the dumplings with a teaspoon of sour cream and sprinkle of chives.

Blended Chilli Tomato topped with Juicy Chicken Dumplings

SERVES 2

Originating in Nepal, you'll also find variations of momo across Tibet, Nepal, Bhutan and India. They're commonly served with a delicately spiced sauce called achaar – a tomato chilli chutney-style sauce – and can be steamed, deep-fried or pan-fried. These moreish dumplings can be filled with all kinds of ingredients and pleated into different sizes. In Tibet, the filling is typically yak or wild Asian ox; however, if your local supermarket is all out of yak ... just go for my lovely chicken alternative instead.

FOR THE DUMPLINGS

200g (7oz) plain (all-purpose) flour, plus extra for dusting
¼ tsp salt
200g (7oz) chicken mince (ground chicken)
½ red onion, chopped
1 garlic clove, finely chopped or grated
1cm (½in) piece of ginger, grated
1 red chilli, finely chopped
1 spring onion (scallion), finely chopped
15g (½oz) finely chopped coriander (cilantro)
Salt and pepper

FOR THE DIPPING SAUCE

1 tbsp vegetable oil
4 tomatoes, finely chopped
4 garlic cloves
1–2 red chillies, roughly chopped (with the seeds)
2 tbsp light soy sauce
2 tsp black pepper
50ml (generous 2½fl oz) chicken or veg stock
1 tsp sugar

TO GARNISH

Chopped fresh coriander (cilantro)
Sesame seeds

1. Combine the flour and salt in a large bowl, then gently pour in 100ml (3½fl oz) water. Mix together with your hands, a wooden spoon or chopsticks until a rough dough forms. Knead for a minute in the bowl, then cover the bowl with cling film (plastic wrap) and set aside.
2. Add all the remaining dumpling ingredients to another large bowl and season with salt and pepper. Mix thoroughly until a smooth paste has formed.
3. Turn the dough out on to a work surface and poke a hole in the middle with a chopstick, then widen the hole to make a large doughnut with a big hole. Slice the doughnut, form it into a log, then cut the log into 16–20 equal pieces.
4. Dust your surface with flour. Get a piece of dough and flatten it gently with the ball of your hand, then roll out with a rolling pin into a round wrapper around 1–2mm thick (paper thin). Place a heaped teaspoon of the filling into the centre of the wrapper. Then working in a clockwise motion, pinch the edge of the wrapper and fold it over itself, then take the section you have just folded and pinch and fold that section. Keep working around the edge of the wrapper, pinching and sealing as you go to make a whirlpool pattern, until you have come to the end and the dumpling is sealed. Repeat with the remaining pieces of dough and filling.
5. Place the dumplings in a steamer and cook for 6–8 minutes.
6. Meanwhile, make the dipping sauce: add all the ingredients to a frying pan (skillet) and place over a high heat. Fry for 5 minutes, stirring, until the tomatoes have softened. Transfer to a blender and blitz until smooth.
7. Pour the dipping sauce into a serving bowl, then top with the dumplings, fresh coriander and sesame seeds.

SERVES 2–3

Paneer & Potato Dumplings in a Cashew Chickpea Tomato Cream

I love potatoes, cooked in every way. These deep-fried paneer and potato dumplings – little islands in a sea of homemade curry sauce – are inspired by the popular Indian malai kofta. They're crisp on the outside and light on the inside, and are bursting with cumin, ginger and garlic. I've kept the sauce smooth, but if you're keen to bulk up the sauce with other ingredients, I'd recommend adding in some chopped peppers, aubergine (eggplant) or cauliflower.

FOR THE DUMPLINGS

2 potatoes, approx. 350g (12oz),
  scrubbed and quartered
150g (generous 5oz) paneer cheese,
  crumbled
1cm (½in) piece of ginger, grated
2 garlic cloves, finely chopped
  or grated
1 tsp ground cumin
3 tbsp cornflour (cornstarch),
  plus extra as needed
Salt and pepper
Oil, for frying

FOR THE SAUCE

2 tbsp vegetable oil
1 white onion, finely diced
¼ tsp ground cinnamon
¼ tsp ground cloves
1 tsp chilli powder
½ tsp garam masala
1 tsp sugar
400g (14oz) tin chopped tomatoes
75g (2½oz) cashews
100ml (3½fl oz) chicken stock
200ml (7oz) single (light) cream
½ x 400g tin (7oz) chickpeas
  (garbanzo beans), drained and
  rinsed

1. Add the potatoes to a saucepan of salted water and bring to the boil. Once boiling, reduce the heat to a simmer and cook for 5–10 minutes, or until the potatoes are cooked. Drain and set aside in a colander to cool.

2. Meanwhile, make a start on the sauce. Heat the oil in a frying pan (skillet) over a medium heat, add the diced onion and fry for 3 minutes, stirring frequently, then add the ground spices, sugar and salt and pepper. Fry for 1 minute and then add the chopped tomatoes, cashews, chicken stock and cream. Bring to the boil, then reduce the heat to low and leave to simmer for 10 minutes.

3. Back to your dumplings. Transfer the potatoes to a large bowl and mash them. Add the crumbled paneer, ginger, garlic, ground cumin, cornflour and a big pinch of salt and pepper. Mix thoroughly until everything is well combined. It's normal for the dough to stick to your hands a bit; you can dust your hands with cornflour to avoid this. Form the dough into 8 balls, each about the size of a golf ball, using the palm of your hand. Optionally, you can lightly coat the balls in cornflour before frying them too.

4. Place a heavy-based saucepan over a medium heat and pour in enough vegetable oil to come about halfway up the sides. To check if the oil is hot enough, put the handle of a wooden spoon into the oil; if bubbles form around it, it's ready.

TO SERVE

2 tbsp cashews

Chopped fresh coriander (cilantro)

50ml (generous 2½fl oz) single (light)
cream

5. Use a slotted spoon to gently lower the dumplings into the oil. Fry for 3–5 minutes on each side or until the dumplings are golden. Make sure to move the dumplings around carefully, as you don't want them sticking to the base of the pan. Remove with a slotted spoon and set aside on a plate lined with kitchen paper (kitchen towel).

6. Next up, using a hand-held blender (or by transferring the sauce to a blender), blitz the sauce until smooth. Taste and adjust the seasoning. Add the chickpeas to the sauce and then simmer over a low heat for a couple of minutes to warm them through.

7. Pour the sauce on to your serving dish and top with the dumplings. Scatter over the cashews and coriander and drizzle over the cream.

SERVES 4

Chilli Chicken & Sweet Potato Peanut Stew with Fluffy Balls

Botswana, renowned for its breathtaking landscapes, also holds a culinary gem: madombi. These large and airy leavened dumplings are made by hand, then delicately cooked on top of a stew until they have ballooned in size. I've scattered chillies into the dumpling dough but feel free to remove them if you're not a fan of spice. The crowd-pleasing stew features tender chicken and sweet potato as its hearty base, complemented by a medley of peanuts, tomatoes and aromatic herbs for seasoning.

FOR THE DUMPLINGS

200g (7oz) plain (all-purpose) flour, plus extra for dusting
1 tbsp baking powder
1 tsp salt
2 mild chillies, deseeded and finely chopped (optional)
1 tsp active dry yeast
1 tsp sugar
100ml (3½fl oz) warm water

FOR THE STEW

1 tbsp olive oil
4 skinless chicken thigh fillets, sliced
1 onion, finely diced
2 garlic cloves, minced
2.5cm (1in) piece of ginger, grated
½ tbsp chilli flakes
1 sweet potato (about 350g), peeled and chopped into bite-sized chunks
75g (2½oz) tomato purée
100g (3½oz) peanut butter
400g (14oz) tin chopped tomatoes
1 tbsp brown sugar
Salt and pepper

TO SERVE

Mild green chilli, thinly sliced
Peanuts, crushed

1. Add the flour, baking powder, salt, mild chillies (if using), yeast and sugar to a bowl and whisk together. Gradually pour in the warm water, mixing at the same time, until a rough sticky dough has formed.
2. Transfer the dough to a lightly floured work surface and knead for 1 minute until smooth and bouncy – add more flour if it's sticking to your hands. Place the dough back into the bowl and cover the dish with a damp cloth or cling film (plastic wrap) and leave to rise in a warm dry area for 1 hour.
3. When the dough has rested for about 15 minutes, make a start on the stew. Heat the olive oil in a large saucepan over a medium heat and add the sliced chicken. Fry for a few minutes and then add the onion, garlic and ginger. Fry for 5 minutes until the onion is soft, then add the chilli flakes, sweet potato, tomato purée and peanut butter and cook, stirring, for a further 2 minutes.
4. Add the chopped tomatoes, brown sugar and 400ml (13½fl oz) water and season with salt and pepper. Bring to the boil, reduce the heat, cover with a lid and leave to simmer for 30 minutes, or until your dough has risen. Taste and adjust the seasoning.
5. Once your dough has doubled in size and your sweet potato is soft, check the stew again; if it's looking a bit dry, add another 200ml (7fl oz) water and give everything a mix.
6. Divide the dough into 8 equal portions and then roll into balls. Carefully place the balls of dough on top of the stew and cover with the lid. Cook over a low heat for 25–30 minutes, or until the dumplings have doubled in size and are light and fluffy.
7. Serve the stew and dumplings topped with sliced green chilli and crushed peanuts.

'Nduja & Cream Cheese Stuffed Squares with a Cherry Tomato Sauce

SERVES 2

We have the Italians to thank for the marvellous dish that is ravioli. This may sound silly, but I often feel underwhelmed when eating it out in restaurants. Unlike most pasta dishes, where you feel full and satisfied after a hearty serving, a mere three to five pieces of ravioli doesn't do the trick for me. So, I make it at home quite often instead, and give myself a generous portion. Which is exactly what I'm offering you in this dish. Simmered gently in a homemade cherry tomato sauce, these rich and moreish pasta pockets are totally and utterly delicious.

FOR THE DUMPLINGS

200g (7oz) '00' flour, plus extra
 for dusting
2 eggs
1 tbsp olive oil
1 tbsp 'nduja paste
200g (7oz) ricotta cheese, drained
 of excess liquid
10 sun-dried tomatoes, finely
 chopped
1 tbsp grated Parmesan cheese
Salt and pepper

FOR THE CHERRY TOMATO SAUCE

2 tbsp olive oil
500g (1lb 2oz) cherry tomatoes
3 garlic cloves, finely chopped
 or grated
1 tbsp balsamic vinegar
½ tsp sugar
Salt and pepper

TO SERVE

Grated Parmesan cheese
Torn basil leaves

1. Add the flour, eggs and olive oil to a bowl and mix until a rough dough forms. If the dough is way too dry, add a splash of water. Turn the dough out on to a floured work surface and knead for 2 minutes, then place the dough in a clean bowl and cover with cling film (plastic wrap). Rest for 30 minutes in the fridge while you make the filling and sauce.

2. Combine the 'nduja paste, drained ricotta, sun-dried tomatoes and grated Parmesan in a bowl and season to taste with salt and pepper. Set aside.

3. Next up, make your sauce. Place a large frying pan (skillet) over a low heat and drizzle in the olive oil. Add the cherry tomatoes, cover with the lid and leave to cook for 5 minutes, then remove the lid and gently press down on the cherry tomatoes to squish them. Add the garlic, balsamic vinegar and sugar and season generously with salt and pepper. Pour in 100ml (3½fl oz) water and leave to simmer while you make your pasta dough. Keep checking on it – you want it to be saucy, but not too liquidy.

4. Time to roll out your dough. You can either use a rolling pin or a pasta machine if you have one! Dust your work surface or pasta machine with flour to prevent sticking.

5. Cut the pasta dough in half and then gently roll it out into a very thin sheet (around 1mm thick – paper thin) or feed it through your pasta roller, starting on the bigger section, and then slowly going down to the smaller settings. Fold the dough into a rectangle after the dough has been rolled through twice, to make it easier for you to roll. Continue to roll

the pasta dough through your machine, dusting with flour in between just in case the pasta gets sticky. The pasta sheet is ready when it's slightly translucent. You're looking for a long, thin rectangular-shaped sheet of pasta dough that you can then dot your filling down the centre.

6. Place your pasta sheet on a floured surface and then roll out the other piece of dough. Place teaspoons of the filling down the centre of the sheet, spaced 5cm (2in) apart. Place the second sheet on top, and gently press around the fillings, making little mounds in the dough. Cut the ravioli out of the dough sheets, forming them into little 5–8cm (2–3in) squares.

7. Bring a saucepan of salted water to the boil, then reduce the heat to a gentle simmer. Carefully lower in the ravioli and cook for 3 minutes. Remove the cooked ravioli with a slotted spoon and transfer to your pan of tomato sauce. Gently mix and combine over a low heat for 1 minute.

8. Divide the ravioli and sauce between plates and top with grated Parmesan and fresh basil.

Chickpea & Sautéed Onion Dumplings with a Ginger Carrot Dressing

SERVES 2

This recipe is a take on the vegetarian Armenian manti dumplings, which I've filled with spiced chickpeas and served with a simple carrot and ginger dressing. Garnished with single cream and pumpkin seeds for a bit of crunch, the flavours in this dish are fresh and zingy.

FOR THE DUMPLINGS

200g (7oz) flour, plus extra for
    dusting
½ tsp fine sea salt
1 medium egg
1 tbsp olive oil
1 onion, chopped
200g (7oz) tinned/jarred chickpeas
    (garbanzo beans), drained
    and rinsed
1 tsp paprika
1 tbsp chopped parsley
Salt and pepper

FOR THE DRESSING

10g (scant ½oz) grated ginger
½ tbsp honey
½ tbsp soy sauce
Juice of 1 lime
½ tsp salt
100ml (3½fl oz) olive oil
1 large carrot, peeled and finely
    grated

TO SERVE

Single (light) cream
Sunflower seeds
Parsley

1. Combine the flour and sea salt in a large bowl, then add the egg and 50ml (scant 2fl oz) water and mix until a shaggy dough forms. Knead in the bowl until you have a rough dough – if the dough sticks to your hands, add more water (you can also knead this on a floured surface). Cover the bowl with cling film (plastic wrap) and set aside while you prepare the filling.

2. Heat the olive oil in a frying pan (skillet) over a medium heat, add the onion and fry for 5 minutes until soft. Meanwhile, add the chickpeas to another bowl and mash with the back of a fork. Add the softened onions, paprika, parsley and salt and pepper. Combine thoroughly and set aside.

3. Next up, get your dough and give it another knead for about 30 seconds on a clean surface. Poke a hole through the centre of the dough and then widen the hole, forming a large doughnut. Slice the doughnut into 16–20 pieces.

4. On a floured surface, roll each piece of dough out into a round wrapper about 2mm thick (paper thin) and 8–10cm (3–4in) in diameter. Place a teaspoon of the filling into the centre of the wrapper and then bring up two opposite corners and lightly pinch in the middle. On one side, crimp inwards, towards the centre of the dumpling four times. Then swizzle the dumpling around and do the same on the other side. You should end up with a wavy dumpling (see pages 32–33). Repeat for all the dumplings.

5. Place the dumplings in a steamer (brushed with oil if it's a metal one) and steam for 6 minutes.

6. Meanwhile, in a bowl combine the ginger, honey, soy sauce, lime juice, salt and 25ml (1fl oz) water to make the dressing. Whisk in the oil and then stir in the grated carrots. Heat in the microwave (with a lid so it doesn't splatter everywhere) for 2 minutes, or until piping hot. Alternatively transfer to a small saucepan and place over a low heat for a couple of minutes.

7. Divide the dressing between plates and top with your dumplings. Drizzle over the cream, and top with sunflower seeds and parsley.

Deep-fried Beef & Parsley Nibbles

Rissóis de carne, the Portuguese snack of little deep-fried breaded dough parcels stuffed with meat, are the inspiration for this dish. Deep-frying is the traditional way of cooking these, but if you have one an air fryer is a great way to get similar results (using a fraction of the oil). There's no need for a dipping sauce; they're great on their own and the fatty beef mince provides enough moisture! Of all the dumplings I've made these are my dad's favourite.

FOR THE DOUGH
1 tbsp butter
1 tbsp olive oil
Pinch of salt
200g (7oz) plain (all-purpose) flour, plus extra for dusting

FOR THE FILLING
Drizzle of olive oil
½ onion, finely chopped
2 garlic cloves, finely chopped or grated
1 tsp paprika
200g (7oz) 20% fat beef mince (ground beef)
15g (½oz) roughly chopped parsley
2 tbsp tomato purée
1 tbsp plain (all-purpose) flour
1–2 tbsp beef stock
Salt and pepper

FOR FRYING
3 tbsp plain (all-purpose) flour
2 eggs, beaten
350g (12oz) breadcrumbs
Vegetable oil

1. To make the dough, place a saucepan over a medium heat and add the butter, olive oil, salt and 150ml (5fl oz) water. Bring to the boil, then reduce the heat to low, add the flour and whisk until a smooth dough forms.

2. Transfer the dough ball to a floured surface; once cool enough to touch, knead the dough for a few minutes. Sprinkle with flour if the dough is sticking to your hands, you want a soft but non-sticky dough. Once again, sprinkle with flour, wrap in cling film (plastic wrap) and set aside to cool.

3. To make the filling, place a frying pan (skillet) over a medium heat and drizzle with oil. Add the onion, garlic and paprika and fry for a few minutes. Add the beef and fry for another 5 minutes. Add the parsley, tomato purée and flour, give everything a stir, then add the beef stock and stir until thickened. Season with salt and pepper and remove from the heat.

4. Get your dough and roll it out on a floured surface to a thickness of about 4mm (generous ⅛in). Using a 10cm (4in) cookie cutter (or large glass), cut out round wrappers from the dough.

5. Place a heaped teaspoon of the filling into the centre of each wrapper, then fold over to make a semicircle, sealing with a fork around the edges. Repeat for all the dumplings.

6. When you are ready to fry the dumplings, place the flour in one bowl, the beaten eggs in another and the breadcrumbs in a third. Dip the dumplings in the flour, followed by the egg, followed by the breadcrumbs.

7. Pour enough vegetable oil for deep-frying into a heavy-based saucepan, to come halfway up the sides of the pan. Place it over a medium heat; to check if the oil is hot enough, drop in a breadcrumb: if it sizzles, the oil is ready to go.

8. Gently lower in the dumplings and fry on each side for about 3–5 minutes, or until golden. Remove with a slotted spoon, drain on kitchen paper (kitchen towel) and serve up!

The 'Oooof' Dumpling Soup

SERVES 2–3

For this recipe, I thought it would be fun to borrow the aromatic broth of khao soi (served in parts of Laos, Thailand and Myanmar) and add ginger and garlic dumplings. It's a real party for the senses – hence the chosen name 'oooof'.

FOR THE DUMPLINGS

1 tbsp vegetable oil
5 spring onions (scallions), finely chopped
2 garlic cloves, finely chopped or grated
1cm (½in) piece of ginger, grated
200g (7oz) plain (all-purpose) flour, plus extra for dusting
1 tsp salt
Cornflour (cornstarch), for dusting

FOR THE SOUP

1 red chilli
1 shallot, roughly chopped
3 garlic cloves, peeled
1 lemongrass stick, white part only, rough chopped
Zest and juice of 1 lime
2cm (1in) piece of ginger
15g (½oz) chopped coriander (cilantro)
Pinch of salt
Pinch of sugar
1 tbsp vegetable oil
500ml (generous 1 pint) veggie stock
400ml (14oz) tin coconut milk
2 tbsp light soy sauce
½ tbsp sugar
1 carrot, thinly sliced
2 pak choi, roughly chopped
100g (3½oz) beansprouts

TO SERVE

2–3 lime wedges
½ small red onion, thinly sliced
Chopped fresh coriander (cilantro)
Sesame seeds

1. Heat the oil in a frying pan (skillet) over a medium heat. Add the spring onions, garlic and ginger and fry for 2 minutes, or until aromatic. Turn off the heat and set aside.

2. Tip the flour and salt, into a bowl and add the spring onion mixture and 80ml (scant 3fl oz) water. Use chopsticks, a wooden spoon or your hands and combine until a shaggy dough forms, then tip the dough out on a lightly floured surface and knead for 30 seconds. Wrap in cling film (plastic wrap) and set it aside while you prepare the soup.

3. Put the red chilli, shallot, garlic, lemongrass, lime zest and juice, ginger, coriander, salt and sugar into a blender and blend into a smooth paste. If you're struggling to blend it, add in a few tablespoons of water.

4. Heat the oil in a saucepan over a medium heat, add your paste and fry for 3–5 minutes until fragrant. Add the stock, coconut milk, light soy sauce and sugar and bring to the boil, then reduce heat and simmer for 10 minutes. Taste and adjust the seasoning.

5. Slice the dough ball into 2 equal pieces and roll each one into a 30cm (12in) log.

6. Add the carrots, pak choi and beansprouts to the soup, then gently hold one end of the long dumpling log and dangle it over the soup. Using sharp scissors, starting from the end of the log nearest the broth, cut 2cm (¾in) long pieces into the broth. Repeat for the second log. Cook for 2–3 minutes, or until the dumplings are floating on the surface.

7. Divide the dumpling soup between 2–3 bowls, top with lime wedges, red onion, coriander and sesame seeds.

SPEEDY

EATS

Quick and simple recipes to ease you into dumpling making. This chapter is all about playing with flavours and making something creative with a dumpling, whether they're homemade or store-bought. I won't judge, I just want you to have fun.

10+ MINS

DUMPLINGS

Vibrant Dumpling Chaat

SERVES 2–3

Chaat is one of the many gorgeous snacks that India has to offer. It is a flavour powerhouse that combines an array of ingredients. There are dozens of types of chaat including pani puri, dahi vada and aloo chaat. When we travelled to India, I was blown away by the marriage of flavours in these dishes. I loved samosa chaat – a dish which has inspired this recipe. So, this plate of food lands somewhere between India and Italy, as we are borrowing tortellini for our dumpling element and coating it in chaat's personality. Perfect served with masala chai.

2 tbsp vegetable oil
250g (9oz) or 20 dumplings of your choice (I used spinach and ricotta tortellini)

FOR THE TAMARIND SAUCE
2 tbsp boiling water
1 tbsp tamarind paste (or use the juice of ½ lemon mixed with 1 tbsp light brown sugar)
1 tbsp light brown sugar
½ tsp ground cumin
½ tsp ground ginger

FOR THE GREEN CHUTNEY
10g (scant ½oz) coriander (cilantro)
10g (scant ½oz) mint
1 green chilli
Juice of 1 lime
1 tsp flaky salt

TO SERVE
200g (7oz) plain yoghurt
1 tsp garam masala
½ tsp flaky salt
100g (3½oz) tinned/jarred chickpeas (garbanzo beans)
½ red onion, finely chopped
5 tbsp Bombay mix or nylon sev
3 tbsp pomegranate seeds
Coriander (cilantro) leaves, to serve

1. Heat the oil in a non-stick frying pan (skillet) over a medium heat and carefully add the tortellini, flat side down. Cook for 1–2 minutes until the bottoms of the tortellini are golden. Add about 3 tablespoons water and then place a lid on the pan and cook for 3 minutes, or until the water has evaporated. Turn off the heat and set aside.

2. Meanwhile, combine all the tamarind sauce ingredients in a small bowl. Set aside.

3. Add all the green chutney ingredients to a blender along with 20ml (1fl oz) water and blend until smooth.

4. In a small bowl, combine the plain yoghurt, garam masala and flaky salt. Spread this out evenly on a serving plate.

5. Remove the tortellini from the pan and place on top of the yoghurt followed by the chickpeas. Drizzle over the tamarind sauce and green chutney. Scatter over the chopped red onion, Bombay mix or sev, pomegranate seeds and coriander.

Zingy Tomato & Crispy Dumpling Salad

A fresh tomato salad is an absolute winner on a hot summer's day. But to turn it into a full meal, I need something extra (perhaps that's just me). The answer: dumplings. The combination of juicy tomatoes, crispy warming pockets of joy and a zingy spicy dressing is heaven on a plate. Whip it up in no time and enjoy.

FOR THE DUMPLINGS

2 tbsp vegetable oil
250g (9oz) or 20 dumplings of your choice (I used Japanese gyoza)
300g (10½oz) mixed tomatoes, halved if small or cut into wedges if large
Salt and pepper

FOR THE DRESSING

1 tbsp sugar
1 tbsp fish sauce
1 tbsp lime juice
1 garlic clove, finely chopped or grated
1 tbsp chilli oil
1 tbsp olive oil

TO SERVE

3 tbsp crushed dry-roasted peanuts
3 tbsp store-bought crispy onions
20g (generous ½oz) roughly chopped coriander (cilantro) leaves
20g (generous ½oz) roughly chopped mint leaves

1. Heat the vegetable oil in a large non-stick frying pan (skillet) over a medium heat, then carefully add the dumplings, flat side down, and cook for 1–2 minutes until the bottoms of the dumplings are golden. Add about 75ml (2½fl oz) water, cover the pan with a lid and cook for 6–8 minutes, or until the water has evaporated.
2. Meanwhile, add the chopped tomatoes to a large bowl and season generously with salt and pepper. Toss to combine.
3. To make the dressing, add all the ingredients to a bowl and whisk to combine. Taste and adjust the seasoning to your preference.
4. Once the dumplings are crispy on the bottom, remove them from the pan and transfer to the bowl of chopped tomatoes. Drizzle over the dressing and lightly toss.
5. Arrange the tomato dumpling salad on a serving plate and top with crushed peanuts, crispy onions, coriander and mint.

Steamed Dumplings in a Spicy Tomato Sauce

SERVES 2–3

This is a quick, speedy version for one of my favourite dumpling sauces of all time: momo chutney, a sauce paired with Nepalese momo that are loved and adored across Nepal, Tibet, Bhutan and India. This recipe is my version of a homemade momo chutney, which you can then pair either with homemade momo (see page 141) or store-bought dumplings if you're short on time.

Drizzle of olive oil

3–4 tomatoes, roughly chopped

4 garlic cloves, sliced

1 red chilli, roughly chopped

2 tbsp light soy sauce

1 tsp black pepper

100ml (3½fl oz) vegetable stock

1 tsp sugar

300g (10½oz) vegan dumplings of your choice (I used homemade momo)

1 spring onion (scallion), finely chopped

1. Place a frying pan (skillet) over a medium heat and add a drizzle of oil. Add the chopped tomatoes and fry for a few minutes until soft.

2. Add the garlic, chilli, light soy sauce and black pepper and fry for 2 more minutes, then pour in the vegetable stock and add the sugar. Leave to simmer for 5 minutes, then turn off the heat and set aside.

3. Meanwhile, steam your chosen dumplings for 6–8 minutes.

4. Transfer the tomato sauce to a blender and blitz until smooth, then pour into the base of your serving plates and top with the steamed dumplings. Sprinkle with spring onions and serve immediately.

No-fuss Chicken & Dumpling Soup

SERVES 2–3

I have one word for you: cosy. This recipe makes the perfect bowl of comfort food, with which you can snuggle up on the sofa with a good book and enjoy a peaceful evening. Here you've got the flavours from the American classic chicken and dumplings and textures from Italian gnocchi.

1 tbsp olive oil
2 chicken breasts, thinly sliced
1 carrot, finely chopped
1 leek, trimmed and finely chopped
1 celery stick, finely chopped
2 garlic cloves, finely chopped
  or grated
½ tbsp dried rosemary
½ tbsp dried thyme
1 tbsp butter
1 tbsp plain (all-purpose) flour
300ml (10fl oz) chicken stock
400g (14oz) tin cream of chicken
  soup
1 tsp hot sauce (or use smoked
  paprika)
250g (9oz) gnocchi
Salt and pepper
Chopped parsley, to garnish

1. Heat the oil in a large saucepan over a high heat. Add the sliced chicken and fry for 2 minutes, stirring frequently.
2. Add the carrot, leek, celery, garlic cloves, dried rosemary and thyme and season generously with salt and pepper. Reduce the heat to medium and fry for 3 minutes, stirring occasionally.
3. Add the butter. Once it has melted add the flour and stir to combine. Gradually pour in the chicken stock, stirring often to avoid any lumps. Next, pour in the cream of chicken soup and the hot sauce (or paprika). Bring to the boil and then reduce the heat to medium-low and cook for 5 minutes. Taste and adjust the seasoning.
4. Add the gnocchi and stir gently through; cook for a further 2 minutes.
5. Serve in deep bowls, sprinkle with fresh parsley and enjoy!

Air Fryer Crunchy Dumplings with Green Tahini

SERVES 2–3

If you've never made green tahini before, you're missing out. It's made by blending tahini, spring onions, coriander, lemon juice, maple syrup and garlic – honestly, it's phenomenal. You end up with a sweet, fresh, smoky sauce that pairs perfectly with crispy air fried Asian-style dumplings. The sauce itself is a semi-permanent resident in my fridge as it can be added to the simplest of meals to jazz them up every time.

250g (9oz) or 20 vegan dumplings of your choice (I used potstickers)
Vegetable oil, for brushing
1 tbsp black or white sesame seeds
Coriander (cilantro), to garnish

FOR THE GREEN TAHINI
2 tbsp tahini
Juice of ½ lemon
2 spring onions (scallions), roughly chopped
1 garlic clove
20g (generous ½oz) chopped coriander (cilantro)
1 tbsp maple syrup
1 tsp flaky salt
3 tbsp olive oil

1. Brush your dumplings lightly with vegetable oil, then place them into your air fryer basket and air fry at 180°C/350°F. The cook time can vary depending on your air fryer and the brand you use, but these times are a good starting point: 6–8 minutes for frozen potstickers, 4–5 minutes for fresh or defrosted.

2. Meanwhile, add all the green tahini ingredients to a blender with 5 tablespoons water and blitz until smooth.

3. Pour the green tahini sauce on to a serving plate and top with your air-fried dumplings. Sprinkle with sesame seeds and coriander and enjoy immediately.

Easy Hot & Sour Soup Dumplings

SERVES 2–3

While travelling across China, one of my favourite times of the day was when we'd sit down to eat. One time we were staying at a guest house in Guilin and for breakfast were served a traditional European spread. Don't get me wrong, I love a good old European breakfast but when I saw a couple of the chefs slurp on hot and sour soup, I cheekily asked if I could have that for breakfast instead. To my surprise, they were thrilled that I wanted to swap my bread and jam for their homemade soup ... and of course, I was delighted that they were so happy to give me some. It was the best breakfast I could have had, so I've reimagined my warming breakfast and topped it with some dumplings for extra bite. Have this bowl for breakfast, lunch or dinner – whatever tickles your fancy.

900ml (scant 2 pints) vegetable stock
½ carrot, julienned
6 mushrooms, sliced
250g (9fl oz) or 20 veggie dumplings of your choice (I used bibigo veggie dumplings)
300g (10½oz) silken tofu, cut into bite-sized pieces
2 tbsp cornflour (cornstarch) mixed with 4 tbsp cold water
2 eggs, beaten
Salt
2 spring onions (scallions), finely chopped, to garnish

FOR THE SAUCE
1 garlic clove, grated
5g (¼oz) piece of ginger, grated
4 tbsp light soy sauce
3 tbsp rice wine vinegar
1 tbsp sugar
1 tsp ground black or white pepper

1. Pour the vegetable stock into a large saucepan, add the carrot and mushrooms and bring to the boil, then reduce the heat and simmer for 2 minutes.
2. Carefully add your chosen dumplings and the silken tofu and cook for another 2 minutes over a medium heat.
3. Meanwhile, combine all the sauce ingredients in a small bowl, then pour into the pan and cook for a further 2 minutes. Season to taste with salt.
4. Add the cornflour mixture to the pan and stir for 1 minute until the soup has thickened, then turn off the heat and drizzle in the beaten eggs. Let the eggs sit for 30 seconds before gently mixing everything together.
5. Ladle your dumpling soup into bowls and garnish with the spring onions.

Speedy Harissa Aubergine, Butter Bean & Dumpling Stew

SERVES 2–3

I love aubergine however it's prepared – grilled, steamed, boiled, fried, roasted ... it's all perfect to me. When added to a stew, it provides a meaty, silky bite and absorbs all the juicy flavours surrounding it. Most stews take hours to cook, but this one is a speedy, no-fuss one that becomes a full meal when served with dumplings. The main added flavour is rose harissa paste. Like any paste, the strength of the spice can vary depending on the brand and source so start by adding small spoonfuls of the paste and adjust based on your preferred level of heat!

2 tbsp olive oil

1 large aubergine (eggplant) or 2 small ones, sliced into chunks

2 garlic cloves, thinly sliced

1 tbsp tomato purée

400g (14oz) tin chopped tomatoes

400g (14oz) tinned/jarred butter beans, drained and rinsed

1 tsp sugar

1 tbsp rose harissa paste

250g (9oz) or 20 vegan dumplings of your choice (I used tortellini)

2 tbsp tahini

½ tsp sugar

2 tbsp pine nuts

Salt and pepper

Chopped parsley, to garnish

1. Heat the oil in a large frying pan (skillet) over a medium heat. Add the aubergine and garlic with 4 tablespoons water and cook for 5 minutes, stirring frequently, until the aubergine has softened slightly.
2. Add the tomato purée, chopped tomatoes, butter beans, sugar and harissa and season generously with salt and pepper. Bring the mixture to the boil, then reduce the heat to low and add another 2 tablespoons water. Give everything a mix and then press your dumplings down into the sauce. Cover with a lid and simmer for 6 minutes (or according to the packet instructions).
3. Meanwhile, in a small bowl, combine the tahini and sugar with 3 tablespoons warm water and stir into a smooth sauce.
4. Plate up your harissa bean and dumpling stew and drizzle the tahini sauce over the top. Scatter over the pine nuts, garnish with the parsley and serve immediately.

Crispy Korean-style Dumpling & Soba Noodle Salad

SERVES 2–3

This recipe is inspired by bibim mandu: a sweet, crunchy and spicy Korean dumpling salad. It's the ultimate way to get a fix of veggies, dumplings and saucy flavours all at once. I've used some leftover Korean-inspired mandu (see page 53) for this recipe but if you're short on time, feel free to go to your local Asian supermarket and grab any mandu-style dumplings you fancy! I've also added my favourite soba noodles to provide more bulk to the recipe. It's honestly one of my favourite speedy lunches.

2 tbsp vegetable oil

150g (generous 5oz) or 15 vegan dumplings of your choice (I used bibigo mandu)

200g (7oz) noodles

100g (3½oz) red cabbage, thinly sliced

½ cucumber, peeled into ribbons

½ carrot, peeled into ribbons

100g (3½oz) edamame beans

1 tbsp sesame seeds

FOR THE DRESSING

1 tbsp gochujang

2 tbsp rice wine vinegar

1 tbsp light soy sauce

1 tbsp sesame oil

1 tbsp maple syrup

1. Heat the oil in a large non-stick pan over a medium heat. Carefully add the dumplings, flat side down, and cook for 1–2 minutes until the bottoms of the dumplings are golden. Add about 70ml (2½fl oz) water, cover the pan with a lid and cook for 6 minutes. If water still remains in the pan, remove the lid and let the water evaporate so that you get a crispy bottom.

2. Cook the noodles according to the packet instructions, then drain and rinse under cold water. Place them in a large bowl along with the cabbage, cucumber and edamame beans and toss together.

3. Add all the dressing ingredients to a small bowl and whisk to combine.

4. Once your dumplings are cooked, add them to your salad bowl, drizzle over the dressing and toss gently.

5. Pour out your salad on to a serving plate, scatter over the sesame seeds and enjoy!

Chipotle Feta Courgettes with Cannellini Beans & Dumplings

SERVES 2-3

There is so much to be done with courgettes. Their versatility is a gift, and their ability to adapt to a multitude of flavours, textures and ingredients is what makes them such a great vegetable to always have in your fridge. Take these chipotle feta courgettes with cannellini beans and dumplings – a dish full of punchy flavours and spicy notes. The courgettes are chopped at an angle and fried until al dente with garlic and cannellini beans. They are the perfect mediator to balance out the flavours from the tangy feta, spicy chipotle, juicy dumplings and creamy beans.

3 tbsp olive oil

1 courgette (zucchini), chopped in half lengthways and then at an angle into chunks

3 garlic cloves, finely chopped or grated

400g (14oz) tinned/jarred cannellini beans, drained and rinsed

200g (7oz) or 20 vegetarian dumplings of your choice

200ml (7fl oz) vegetable stock

1 tbsp chipotle paste

100g (3½oz) feta cheese, crumbled

Salt and pepper

Chopped parsley, to garnish

1. Heat 2 tablespoons of the olive oil in a large frying pan (skillet) over a medium heat. Add the chopped courgette and season with a teaspoon of flaky salt and several grinds of pepper. Fry for about 3 minutes until coloured on all sides.

2. Add the garlic and cannellini beans and fry for 1 minute, then add your dumplings and the vegetable stock. Cover the pan with a lid, reduce the heat to medium-low and cook for 6–8 minutes.

3. Meanwhile, combine the chipotle paste with the remaining tablespoon of olive oil in a small bowl, adding a splash of water if you want it runnier.

4. Once your dumplings are cooked, transfer your courgettes, beans and dumplings to a serving platter. Top with the crumbled feta, chipotle sauce and chopped parsley. Enjoy!

Homemade Chilli Hummus
with Crispy Lamb & Dumplings

So many cuisines, flavours and ingredients are miles apart, but despite the distance, when combined they can create a unique flavour profile that regularly blows me away. Just like this universally loved Middle Eastern hummus paired with crispy lamb and Chinese-style jiaozi. A cuisine match made in heaven.

SERVES 2–3

1 tbsp olive oil, plus extra for drizzling

1 tbsp cumin seeds

200g (7oz) lamb mince (ground lamb)

½ tbsp smoked paprika

200g (7oz) or 15 dumplings of your choice (I used potstickers)

Salt and pepper

Sliced red chilli and chopped coriander (cilantro), to garnish

FOR THE HUMMUS

400g (14oz) tinned/jarred chickpeas (garbanzo beans), not drained

1 garlic clove

3 tbsp tahini

Juice of 1 lemon

1 tsp ground cumin

1 red chilli, deseeded (if you prefer less heat)

1. Heat the olive oil in a frying pan (skillet) over a high heat, add the cumin seeds and fry for 20 seconds, then add the lamb mince and break it up with a spatula.

2. Add the smoked paprika and season with a pinch salt and pepper. Stir frequently and fry for 10 minutes until the lamb is slightly crispy.

3. Get your steamer ready and place your dumplings inside. Steam for 6–8 minutes.

4. Meanwhile, put the chickpeas, including the liquid (aquafaba) from the jar, into a food processor along with the garlic, tahini, lemon juice, ground cumin, red chilli and a pinch of salt and pepper. Blend until smooth. If you like your hummus super smooth you can add a couple of ice cubes and blend for a further 30 seconds. Use a rubber spatula to spoon the hummus on to a serving plate.

5. When your dumplings are ready, place them on top of your hummus, then sprinkle the crispy lamb on top of your dumplings.

6. Garnish with sliced red chilli and chopped coriander and finish with a drizzle of olive oil.

Shiitake Alfredo Dumplings

SERVES 2–3

An authentic alfredo sauce is made using only four ingredients: fettucine, Parmesan, butter and black pepper. However, it's been adapted over the years to include cream, and in my case, garlic, transforming it into an unctuous and very slightly addictive sauce. For the dumpling addition, aka your fettucine replacement, I had some leftover 'nduja and cream cheese ravioli (see page 146) in the freezer that I used. But if you don't have any to hand, store-bought ravioli, tortellini or pierogi will do.

250g (9oz) or 20 dumplings of your choice (I used ravioli)

2 tbsp butter

1 tbsp oil

3 garlic cloves, finely chopped or grated

125g (4½oz) shiitake mushrooms, larger ones sliced and small ones left whole

300ml (10fl oz) single (light) cream

30g (1oz) grated Parmesan cheese, plus extra to serve

Salt and pepper

Chopped fresh parsley, to serve

1. Bring a large saucepan of salted water to the boil. Reduce the heat, add your chosen dumplings and simmer for 6 minutes.

2. Meanwhile, melt the butter in a large frying pan (skillet) over a medium heat and add the oil, followed by the garlic and mushrooms. Fry for 30 seconds until fragrant.

3. Pour in the cream, stirring constantly to stop it catching on the bottom of the pan. When it begins to simmer, reduce the heat to low and stir in the Parmesan and season generously with salt and pepper.

4. Once the dumplings are cooked, use a slotted spoon to transfer them to the pan of sauce and gently stir until they are coated in the sauce.

5. Serve sprinkled with more Parmesan and chopped parsley.

Dumpling Caesar Salad

SERVES 2–3

I feel like every salad lover has their own way of making a Caesar dressing, but whenever I make this Caesar dressing, I always get asked for the recipe. I love a leafy salad, but go up a level, and you've got pasta salad; up another level, and you've got filled-pasta salad. I've called it dumpling Caesar salad, but my recommendation would be to use either tortellini or ravioli, with a reasonably tame filling like spinach and ricotta, as they'll match up best with the flavours of the salad. It's a great dish to make for a work from home lunch, or to serve on a summer's day.

250g (9oz) or 10–15 dumplings of your choice (I used Italian ravioli)

4 rashers of smoked streaky bacon

8 little gem lettuce leaves, finely chopped

300g (10½oz) cherry tomatoes, halved

Parmesan shavings, to garnish

FOR THE DRESSING

2 tbsp mayonnaise

1 tbsp cottage cheese or sour cream

2 tbsp grated Parmesan cheese

1 garlic clove, finely chopped or grated

1 tsp wholegrain mustard

1 tbsp lemon juice

1 anchovy fillet, finely chopped

½ tsp ground black pepper

½ tsp paprika

1 tsp balsamic vinegar

1. Bring a large saucepan of salted water to the boil, then reduce the heat to medium. Add the ravioli and cook according to the packet instructions. Drain and set aside.

2. Meanwhile, place a non-stick frying pan (skillet) over a medium heat and add the streaky bacon. Fry on each side for 4 minutes, or until crispy. Transfer to a chopping board and roughly slice.

3. In a small bowl, combine all of your dressing ingredients. If the dressing is a little too thick feel free to add a tablespoon of olive oil to loosen it up a bit. Taste and adjust the seasoning.

4. Start assembling your salad in a large bowl. Combine your chopped salad leaves, bacon pieces and chopped tomatoes, then add the cooked ravioli. Drizzle over the dressing, gently toss everything together and then finish with a few shavings of Parmesan.

Sweet 'Nduja Dumplings with Aubergine & Yoghurt

SERVES 2–3

For those of you who don't know, 'nduja is a spreadable, slightly spicy pork sausage from southern Italy. It's become very popular with its unique kick and bright red colour. It's a condiment that can be used in pasta sauces, spread in sandwiches or dabbed on to a potato frittata, but my favourite use of all is using it as an oil drizzle, adding a punch of flavour to these fried aubergines, dumplings and lemony yoghurt.

4 tbsp olive oil

2 aubergines (eggplants), sliced into 1cm (½in) thick discs, then into thirds

2 tbsp 'nduja

2 tbsp honey

250g (9oz) dumplings of your choice (I used Polish pierogi)

1 garlic clove, finely chopped or grated

250g (9oz) thick yoghurt

Juice of ½ lemon

Salt and pepper

Chopped parsley, to garnish (optional)

1. Heat 2 tablespoons of the olive oil in a large frying pan (skillet) over a medium heat. Add the aubergine pieces with a big pinch of salt and grind of pepper, place a lid on the pan and leave to fry for 3 minutes on one side.

2. Combine the 'nduja, honey and remaining 2 tablespoons olive oil in a small bowl. Heat for 30 seconds in the microwave to loosen the sauce. (Alternatively heat in a small saucepan over a low heat.)

3. Flip the aubergines over and add the dumplings to the pan. Pour 80ml (scant 3fl oz) water and half of your 'nduja sauce over the aubergines and dumplings, place the lid back on the pan and cook for a further 3 minutes.

4. Meanwhile, add the garlic, yoghurt and lemon juice to a bowl and stir to combine. Season to taste with salt and pepper, then spread it over a serving plate.

5. Once your aubergines and dumplings are cooked, gently arrange them on top of the yoghurt and drizzle over the rest of the 'nduja sauce. Scatter over the chopped parsley (if using) and enjoy!

Salsa Verde Dumplings

SERVES 2–3

Salsa verde isn't exclusive to one country. Most places have their own version of it: 'green sauce', from French sauce verte, to Spanish, Mexican and Italian salsa verde, to Yemeni zhoug ... the list goes on. Here I've created a version inspired by Mexican flavours using coriander, green chilli, garlic and lime. The sauce is blended and then fried with your dumplings of choice and eggs – and served with ripe avocado, crumbled feta and fresh coriander. It's a really quick and easy dish to make, but packed full of vibrancy and yumminess.

200g (7oz) or 20 dumplings
  of your choice
2–3 eggs
1 avocado, sliced
100g (3½oz) feta cheese, crumbled
Salt and pepper
Finely chopped coriander (cilantro),
  to garnish

FOR THE SALSA VERDE
30g (1oz) fresh coriander (cilantro)
1 green chilli
1 garlic clove, peeled
50ml (scant 2fl oz) olive oil
Juice of 1 lime
1 tsp sea salt flakes
½ tsp sugar

1. Start with the salsa verde: put all of the ingredients into a blender and blitz until nearly smooth.
2. Place a large non-stick frying pan (skillet) over a medium-low heat. Pour in the salsa, add 50ml (scant 2fl oz) water and bring to a simmer. Add your chosen dumplings, cover the pan with a lid and cook the dumplings for 4 minutes.
3. Remove the lid, crack the eggs into the pan and replace the lid for another 2–3 minutes, or until the whites are set but the yolks are still runny.
4. Season the eggs with salt and pepper, then slide the dumplings, salsa and eggs out of the pan and on to a serving plates. Top with the sliced avocado and crumbled feta cheese and garnish with chopped coriander.

Speedy Laksa-style Dumpling Noodle Soup

SERVES 2–3

Laksa is a popular South East Asian noodle soup prepared with a rich, aromatic and spicy coconut broth. I've had my fair share of laksa and never get bored of the flavours. This recipe is bulked out with prawns, dumplings (you can use the recipe on page 123 or use your favourite store-bought Asian-style dumplings) and the classic wide rice noodles, then top with a jammy egg, a wedge of lime and coriander.

2 garlic cloves
1 red chilli
1 shallot, peeled
2.5cm (1in) piece of ginger
1 lemongrass stick, top and tailed and bashed
200g (7oz) wide/thick rice noodles
2 tbsp vegetable oil
2 tbsp laksa paste or Thai red curry paste
400ml (13½fl oz) chicken stock
400ml (13½fl oz) coconut milk
2 tbsp fish sauce
1 tsp sugar
250g (9oz) or 15 dumplings of your choice
200g (7oz) raw king prawns (shrimp)

TO SERVE
Soft-boiled eggs
Lime wedges
Coriander (cilantro) leaves
Sliced red chilli

1. Begin by putting the garlic cloves, red chilli, shallot, ginger and lemongrass into a blender. Blitz until you have a rough paste (add some oil or water if it's struggling to blend).

2. Cook the noodles according to the packet instructions. Once cooked, drizzle with a bit of vegetable oil so they don't stick together, and then leave in a colander covered with a tea towel so they gently steam.

3. Now is a good time to cook the eggs in boiling water for 6 minutes. Put them in a bowl of cold water until cool enough to handle, then peel them.

4. Place a large saucepan over a medium heat and drizzle in the vegetable oil. Add your aromatic paste and stir-fry for 3 minutes – the smells will be unreal! Now add the laksa or Thai red curry paste, fry for another minute, then add the chicken stock, coconut milk, fish sauce and sugar. Bring to the boil and then reduce to a simmer.

5. Add your chosen dumplings and cook for 2 minutes, then add the prawns and cook for a further 5 minutes. Taste your broth and season according to your preferences.

6. Divide the noodles into bowls, then top with the broth, dumplings and prawns. Garnish each bowl with a jammy soft-boiled egg, a wedge of lime, coriander and red chilli.

SWEET TREATS

There are dozens of sweet dumplings that I could have used as inspiration for this chapter, but I've managed to whittle it down to ten of my favourites. I don't have a huge sweet tooth, so trust me when I say that they will get anyone going.

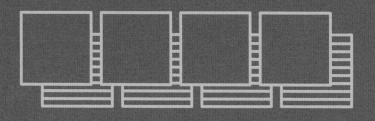

Surprise Apricot Bombs

I love a dessert with a cheeky surprise in the middle, and this one always gets people smiling. The much-loved Austrian marillenknödel is the inspiration for this dish: a cream cheese dough encases an apricot delight and is coated in sweet cinnamon breadcrumbs. In the traditional recipe the dumplings are boiled and then coated in cinnamon breadcrumbs; however, I find that baking them leads to a softer apricot.

FOR THE DUMPLINGS

3 tbsp softened butter
½ tbsp granulated sugar
1 tsp vanilla extract
150g (generous 5oz) cream cheese
1 egg
150g (5oz) plain (all-purpose) flour, plus extra for dusting
Pinch of salt
4 large or 6 small ripe apricots
4 sugar cubes

FOR THE COATING

50g (scant 2oz) butter, plus extra for greasing
50g (scant 2oz) breadcrumbs
1 tsp ground cinnamon
1 tbsp soft light brown sugar

TO SERVE

Icing (powdered) sugar
150ml (5fl oz) custard (optional)

1. Add the butter, sugar and vanilla extract to a bowl and whisk with a hand-held electric whisk until well combined. Add the cream cheese and the egg and whisk until there are no lumps.
2. Add the flour and salt and combine using a wooden spoon until a soft dough forms – add more flour if it sticks to your hands. Cover the bowl with cling film (plastic wrap) and place in the fridge while you prepare the apricots and cinnamon coating.
3. Use a sharp knife to cut the apricots almost in half – just enough so that you can remove the stone. Push a cube of sugar into the cavity left by the stone and set aside while you prepare the breadcrumb coating.
4. Place a frying pan (skillet) over a medium heat and add the butter; once melted, add the breadcrumbs and fry for a few minutes until they're lightly golden. Transfer to a bowl, add the sugar and cinnamon and set aside.
5. Preheat the oven to 180°C/350°F and lightly grease a baking dish with butter.
6. Turn the dough out on to a lightly floured work surface and form into a ball, then cut it into 4 equal pieces. Roll out a piece of dough into a circle that is about 5mm (¼in) thick and large enough to fully wrap your apricot. Place the apricot in the middle of the wrapper and fold the dough up around the apricot, sealing at the top. Repeat to make 4 dumplings.
7. Gently toss the dumplings in the sugar cinnamon mixture until they are coated all over, then add them to the baking dish. Cover with foil and bake for 20 minutes, then remove the foil and bake for another 15 minutes.
8. Dust the dumplings with a sprinkling of icing sugar and serve with custard, if liked.

Maple Syrup & Bacon Bake

SERVES 4

Maple syrup and bacon are an iconic duo that work with so many things, including this sweet dumpling recipe. The dumplings are baked in the oven, gently expanding as they soak up the maple butter syrup, and then served with crispy bacon to give a hit of saltiness and sweet vanilla ice cream. It's essentially a dumplified version of bacon and maple syrup waffles, and it's really really good.

FOR THE DUMPLINGS

250g (9oz) plain (all-purpose) flour, plus extra for dusting
1 tbsp baking powder
1 tsp caster (superfine) sugar
½ tsp salt
½ tsp ground cinnamon
50g (scant 2oz) butter, melted
125ml (4fl oz) milk

TO BAKE THE DUMPLINGS

100ml (3½fl oz) maple syrup
4 tsp butter, melted

TO SERVE

4 rashers of bacon
Vanilla ice cream

1. Preheat the oven to 190°C/375°F.
2. In a large bowl, combine flour, baking powder, sugar, salt and ground cinnamon in a large bowl, then add the melted butter and milk. Mix until a rough dough forms. It shouldn't be super sticky, but it's good if some of the dough is sticking to your hands. You want a light but slightly firm dough.
3. Form the dough into 8 equal-sized balls – dust your hands with a little flour if the dough is sticking to your hands.
4. Get a large baking dish and pour in the maple syrup, melted butter and 150ml (5fl oz) water. Add the dumpling balls, evenly spaced apart, cover the dish with foil or a lid and bake in the oven for 25 minutes. Remove the foil or lid and return to the oven for another 5 minutes.
5. Meanwhile, place a non-stick frying pan (skillet) over a medium heat and add the bacon rashers. Cook for 5–10 minutes until cooked and crispy. Remove and roughly chop the bacon into small pieces.
6. Remove the dumplings from the oven and serve in bowls with a scoop of vanilla ice cream on the side and sprinkled with bacon pieces.

Mini Biscoff Fried Dumplings

While I was travelling across Brazil, it became abundantly clear that the locals love their deep-fried dough balls covered in cinnamon sugar: a dish called bolinhos de chuva. Frequently served with a chocolate dip or dulce de leche, people would eat these for breakfast or as an afternoon snack. My variation of this sweet snack fills the dough with Biscoff spread, which offers a similar flavour to their usual pairings because it's made from caramelized biscuits. You can opt not to stuff them and just melt the Biscoff and use it as a dip, but I love the way the filling oozes out of the deep-fried dough when warm. Very moreish and very tasty!

FOR THE DUMPLINGS

200g (7oz) plain (all-purpose) flour, plus extra for dusting
2 tsp baking powder
25g (scant 1oz) caster (superfine) sugar
½ tsp salt
1 egg
1 tbsp melted butter
50ml (scant 2fl oz) milk
8–10 tbsp Biscoff spread, chilled
Vegetable oil, for frying

TO SERVE

2 tbsp caster (superfine) sugar
1 tbsp ground cinnamon

1. Whisk the flour, baking powder, sugar and salt together in a large bowl. Add the egg, butter and milk and stir using your hands or a wooden spoon until you have a rough dough. Turn out on to a floured surface and knead for 1 minute – add more flour if the dough is sticking to your hands.

2. Divide the dough into 8–10 pieces and then gently roll out each piece into a round wrapper about 8cm (3in) in diameter and 5mm (¼in) thick. Place a heaped teaspoon of Biscoff spread in the centre and gently bring up the sides of the dough around the Biscoff spread. Pinch and twist to seal and remove any excess dough. Roll into a ball and then set aside. Repeat for all the dumplings.

3. Pour about 10cm (4in) of vegetable oil into a large saucepan and heat over a low-medium heat. To check if the oil is hot enough, drop in a little piece of dough; if it sizzles, it's ready. Make sure you heat the oil up slowly and keep an eye on the temperature – if the oil is too hot, it will just burn the dumplings.

4. Line a plate with kitchen paper (kitchen towel) and combine the sugar and cinnamon in a shallow bowl.

5. Carefully lower in the dumplings with a slotted spoon and deep-fry for 4–6 minutes, flipping halfway, until golden brown. You may need to work in batches to avoid overcrowding the pan.

6. Using a slotted spoon, remove the dumplings from the oil and transfer to the paper-lined plate to drain any excess oil. While the dumplings are still hot, toss them in the cinnamon sugar and serve immediately.

Ginger Ale Baked Apple & Blackberry Dumplings

I've tried several ways of making baked apple dumplings, but this version always comes out on top. The secret ingredient is the ginger ale, which is poured into the dish and then absorbed by the dumplings as they bake. You get hints of sweet ginger seeping through the dough, which pairs brilliantly with the robust flavour of the apple and tanginess of the blackberries.

FOR THE DUMPLINGS

200g (7oz) plain (all-purpose) flour, plus extra for dusting
2 tsp baking powder
½ tsp salt
100g (3½oz) unsalted butter, cubed
1 egg
50ml (scant 2fl oz) milk
3 apples, peeled and quartered, core removed
150g (generous 5oz) blackberries
½ tsp ground cinnamon
1 tbsp caster (superfine) sugar
200ml (7fl oz) ginger ale/beer
Ice cream or custard, to serve

1. In a large bowl, whisk together the flour, baking powder and salt. Add the cubed butter and use your fingertips to rub the butter into the flour until it looks like breadcrumbs. Add the egg and milk and mix with a spatula until you have a soft but not sticky dough.

2. Turn the dough out on to a floured surface and knead gently for 30 seconds. Return to the bowl, cover with cling film (plastic wrap) and put into the fridge while you prepare the apples.

3. Preheat the oven to 180°C/350°F.

4. Remove the dough from the fridge and cut it into 12 equal pieces. Roll out each piece into an oval shape big enough to wrap around your apple wedges and about 4mm (¼in) in thickness.

5. One by one, place an apple wedge at the bottom of the wrapper, then tuck and roll the wrapper around the apple and pinch to seal. Repeat to make 12 apple dumplings. Arrange the dumplings in a baking dish and dot the blackberries around the dumplings.

6. Combine the ground cinnamon and sugar in a small bowl, then sprinkle this over the dumplings.

7. Pour the ginger ale around – but not on top of – the dumplings (you don't want them to get soggy). Bake for 35–40 minutes, or until the dumplings are golden brown.

8. Serve warm with ice cream or custard.

Cottage Cheese, Almond & Orange Dumplings

Cottage cheese is one of my favourite ingredients to use at the moment, and so I'm combining it with almond flour and the citrussy flavour of orange to bring you these moreish dumplings. They're based on a Hungarian dumpling called túrógombóc – light, slightly fluffy and perfect for an evening of wholesome food.

FOR THE DUMPLINGS

1 egg, separated
1 tbsp caster (superfine) sugar
1 tsp vanilla extract
Zest and juice of 1 orange
200g (7oz) cottage cheese, drained
200g (7oz) almond flour
100g (3½ oz) self-raising
    (self-rising) flour
3 tbsp butter
150g (generous 5oz) breadcrumbs

TO SERVE

300g (10oz) sour cream
Zest and juice of ½ orange
½ tbsp honey
Icing (powdered) sugar
1 tbsp toasted almonds

1. Beat the egg yolk with the sugar, vanilla extract and orange zest and juice.
2. In a separate bowl, whisk the egg white with an electric whisk until soft peaks form.
3. Add the drained cottage cheese to the egg yolk mixture, along with the beaten egg white, almond flour and self-raising flour. Combine and mix with a spatula until a rough dough forms. The dough shouldn't stick to your hands so if it does, add a little more almond flour.
4. Cover the bowl with cling film (plastic wrap) and set it aside while you toast the breadcrumbs.
5. Melt the butter in a frying pan (skillet) over a medium heat and add the breadcrumbs. Toast for a couple of minutes, then tip into a shallow bowl.
6. Divide the dough into 12 even-sized portions, then shape each one into a dumpling in the palm of your hands – moisten your hands with water to stop the dough sticking. Toss in the self-raising flour and set aside ready to be cooked.
7. Bring a large saucepan of salted water to a low simmer. Carefully lower in the dumplings and stir to prevent them sticking. Simmer for 8 minutes.
8. Meanwhile, combine the sour cream, orange zest and juice and honey in a small bowl.
9. When the dumplings are ready, remove them from the pan with a slotted spoon and roll them in the breadcrumbs until they're well coated.
10. Serve the dumplings topped with the honey-orange sour cream and sprinkle with icing sugar and toasted almonds.

Tiramisu-style Rice Flour Pillows

I love mochi, Japanese sweet treats made from glutinous rice flour, and I love tiramisu, Italy's favourite coffee dessert. So combining the two for me is a total no-brainer. While these mochi may look intimidating, they're not; in fact, once you've got hold of some glutinous rice flour (from any Asian supermarket), they really are quite simple and satisfying to make. The tiramisu-inspired filling is encased in a chewy, cocoa-infused wrapper. Make these for any coffee lover and they'll be seriously impressed.

FOR THE DOUGH

200g (7oz) glutinous rice flour
65g (scant 2½oz) granulated sugar
40g (1½oz) cornflour (cornstarch), plus extra for dusting
1 tbsp cocoa powder, plus extra for dusting
360ml (12fl oz) full-fat (whole) milk
1 tbsp vegetable oil

FOR THE FILLING

250g (9oz) mascarpone
100ml (3½fl oz) double (heavy) cream
75g (2½oz) icing (powdered) sugar
½ tbsp coffee mixed with ½ tbsp water
½ tsp vanilla extract

FOR THE SPONGE

8 sponge fingers, finely chopped
½ tbsp coffee mixed with 4 tbsp water and 1 tsp sugar

1. Start by making the dough: put the glutinous rice flour, sugar, cornflour and cocoa powder into a large heatproof bowl. Give it a stir, then add the milk and whisk until there are no lumps.
2. Cover the bowl with cling film (plastic wrap) and microwave for 2 minutes on a high heat, then mix using a spatula. Return to the microwave for another 2 minutes, then remove and stir. Keep doing this until the dough is thick and ball-shaped.
3. Once the dough has formed a ball, remove from the large bowl and allow it to cool before wrapping in cling film and setting aside in the fridge while you make the filling.
4. Combine the mascarpone, double cream, icing sugar, coffee and water mixture and the vanilla extract in a large bowl. Whisk by hand or with an electric whisk until the filling thickens and forms stiff peaks.
5. Add the chopped sponge fingers to another bowl and pour over the coffee-water-sugar mixture. Combine well, and then gently fold it into the mascarpone mixture. Set aside.
6. Remove the dough from the fridge and add it to a large bowl with the vegetable oil. Knead the dough in the bowl until the oil is all combined and you have a stretchy, oily dough, then divide into 8 equal portions.
7. Dust your work surface with cornflour. Roll out a piece of dough into a round wrapper 8–10cm (3–4in) in diameter and about 6mm (¼in) thick. Place a tablespoon of the filling into the centre of the wrapper, bring the dough up around the filling and twist and seal at the top, pinching off any remaining dough to seal the dumpling well. Repeat to make 8 dumplings.
8. Lightly dust the mochi dumplings with a little cocoa powder, then place them in little cupcake holders or parchment paper and chill in the fridge until you're ready to serve.

Blueberry & Raisin Parcels with Sour Cream & Flaked Almonds

Blueberries pair perfectly with the subtle sweet tones of raisins. Inspired by the Ukrainian dumpling varenyky (which can be made savoury or sweet), this recipe is a go-to of mine when I'm looking for an impressive yet comforting dessert to share with friends.

FOR THE DUMPLINGS

200g (7oz) plain (all-purpose) flour, plus extra for dusting
½ tsp salt
1 egg
250g (9oz) blueberries
75g (2½oz) raisins
50g (scant 2oz) caster (superfine) sugar
1 tbsp lemon juice
½ tsp ground cinnamon

TO SERVE

2 tbsp butter
1 tsp cornflour (cornstarch)
Sour cream
Flaked almonds

1. Combine the flour, salt, egg and 75ml (2½fl oz) water in a large bowl. Mix with a wooden spoon or your hands until a rough dough forms, then tip out on to a floured surface and knead for 1 minute. Add more flour if the dough is sticking to your hands. Wrap in cling film (plastic wrap) and put into the fridge while you make the filling.

2. Put the blueberries, raisins, sugar, lemon juice and cinnamon into a saucepan and place over a medium heat. Bring to the boil, then simmer for 1 minute. Remove from the heat and set aside.

3. Get your dough out and poke a hole through the centre, then use a chopstick or a wooden spoon handle to widen the hole until you have a large doughnut shape. Cut the doughnut into a log, then roll out the log on a floured surface until it's about 2.5cm (1in) wide. Slice the log into 16–20 pieces, then roll each piece into a round wrapper about 8cm (3in) in diameter and 2mm (scant ⅛in) thick.

4. Use a slotted spoon to spoon a small amount of the filling into the centre of a wrapper (you don't want to add too much liquid or you'll find it hard to seal the dumplings). Fold the wrapper in half and pinch to seal, then use a fork to crimp around the edge of the semicircle. Repeat this step for all the other dumplings. The dumpling filling is also going to be used for a sauce, so don't use it all up.

5. Bring a large saucepan of salted water to the boil, then reduce the heat to a simmer. Gently lower in in your dumplings and cook for 5 minutes.

6. Meanwhile, return the remaining dumpling filling to a low heat. Add in the butter and cornflour and stir until the sauce thickens.

7. Remove the dumplings from the pan with a slotted spoon and place into a serving dish. Top with the blueberry sauce, dollop with sour cream and sprinkle with flaked almonds. Enjoy!

Cardamom & Orange Syrup Dumplings

MAKES 12

Warning: if you like sweet stuff, you're going to love this dessert – imagine soft, light and squidgy spiced milk dumplings soaked in a cardamom and orange syrup. It's my take on gulab jamun, one of my favourite Indian sweets, although here I've added egg to bind the dumplings (eggs aren't a common ingredient for this recipe in India), and orange to add a zesty flavour note. This is a great dish to prepare in advance and store in the fridge if you've got guests coming over.

FOR THE DUMPLINGS

100g (3½oz) milk powder
40g (1½oz) plain (all-purpose) flour
5g (¼oz) ghee, melted
1 egg
3 cardamom pods, seeds removed and crushed
Zest of 1 orange
1 tsp baking powder
Pinch salt
2 tbsp milk, plus more if needed
Vegetable oil, for deep-frying

FOR THE SYRUP

200g (7oz) caster (superfine) sugar
3 cardamom pods, seeds removed and crushed (keep the pods)
Juice of 1 orange

TO SERVE

1 tbsp pistachios, crushed
Zest of 1 orange

1. In a large bowl, mix together the milk powder, plain flour, ghee, egg, crushed cardamom seeds, orange zest, baking powder and salt. Add the milk to moisten the dough and mix again until the dough is soft and smooth. Add a little more milk if the dough feels too dry.

2. Divide the dough into 12 equal-sized portions and roll into balls – they should be about 3cm (1¼in) in diameter. Don't squeeze the dough too much as this will compress the air out of it and make the dumplings dense. Just keep rolling gently between the palms of your hands until no creases are visible on the surface of the dough.

3. Pour about 10cm (4in) of vegetable oil into a large saucepan and place over a low-medium heat. To check if the oil is ready, drop in a small piece of dough: if it begins to sizzle, it's ready.

4. Gently lower the dumplings into the oil and fry for 10 minutes, or until golden brown, flipping halfway. Remove with a slotted spoon and drain on a plate lined with kitchen paper (kitchen towel). You may need to deep-fry these in batches.

5. Meanwhile, make the syrup: place another saucepan or large frying pan over a medium heat and add the caster sugar, 400ml (13½fl oz) water, the cardamom crushed seeds and their pods and the orange juice. Bring to the boil and then turn off the heat and leave to cool.

CONTINUES OVERLEAF →

CONTINUES
FROM PAGE 194

6. Using a toothpick, prick holes in the dumplings – this will allow them to soak up more of the sugar syrup.

7. Once your cardamom orange sugar syrup has cooled, transfer the dumplings into the sugar syrup and leave to soak for at least 15 minutes – although the longer you leave them to soak, the better the flavour! If you're making these in advance you could transfer them to a large container with a lid and store them in the fridge until needed.

8. Serve these hot (by warming them up in a pan) or cold, topped with crushed pistachios and orange zest.

Nostalgic Lemon Dumplings

SERVES 6

My all-time favourite dessert is probably my mum's upside-down lemon pudding. Her granny taught it to her, and it's been passed down the generations because it is SO good. It's not traditionally a dumpling, but as this is my first cookbook, I just knew I had to find a way to dumplify the recipe for you all to enjoy. Served in individual portions, little baked lemon dumplings are topped with a simple lemon curd cream, desiccated coconut and mint leaves. It's unbelievably indulgent and pretty addictive, but a great one to serve any sweet-toothed friends.

FOR THE DUMPLINGS

200g (7oz) self-raising (self-rising) flour, plus extra for dusting
180g (6½oz) Greek yoghurt
Zest of 1 lemon and 2 tbsp juice
2 tbsp caster (superfine) sugar
½ tsp fine salt

TO SERVE

300ml (10fl oz) double (heavy) cream
200g (7oz) lemon curd
10g (scant ½oz) desiccated coconut
Fresh mint leaves

1. Combine all the dumpling ingredients together in a large bowl. Mix with your hands or a spoon until a rough dough forms.
2. Tip the dough out on to a floured surface and lightly knead for 1 minute – dusting with flour if it sticks to your hands.
3. Prepare a steamer. Divide the dough into 12 equal-sized balls, then place the dumplings into the steamer, each one on a little circle of baking paper. Steam over a medium-high heat for 6 minutes.
4. Meanwhile, whip the double cream in a large bowl until thick. Fold in half the lemon curd.
5. Once the dumplings are cooked, place them in individual bowls. Pour over the lemon curd topping, add a dollop of the remaining lemon curd and gently swirl through to create a pretty pattern.
6. Sprinkle over the desiccated coconut and fresh mint leaves.

Chocolate Spiral Buns

SERVES 4

I don't really need to tell you how good homemade hot chocolate is, nor will I blabber on about how well it goes with these Chinese-style 'mantou' steamed dumplings. But on second thoughts, maybe I will. Picture this: you're in a Parisian bar, sipping on a mug of thick hot chocolate. However, instead of dipping a flaky croissant into your hot choccie, you're rapidly transported to a Chinese bakery, where you delicately dip your fluffy, cocoa-infused steamed bun instead. Comforting? Yes. Happiness-inducing? Absolutely. It's the perfect pairing for a cold winter's day.

FOR THE DUMPLINGS

150g (generous 5oz) plain (all-purpose) flour, plus extra for dusting
10g (scant ½oz) cornflour (cornstarch)
1 tsp active dry yeast
3 tbsp caster (superfine) sugar
¼ tsp salt
75ml (2½fl oz) warm milk
1 tbsp vegetable oil
7g (¼oz) cocoa powder

FOR THE HOT CHOCOLATE

150ml (5fl oz) single (light) cream
300ml (10fl oz) milk
200g (7oz) milk chocolate, finely chopped
50ml (scant 2fl oz) double (heavy) cream, whipped

1. Combine the plain flour, cornflour, yeast, sugar and salt in a large bowl. Slowly add the warm milk and vegetable oil and mix to combine, then knead the dough for a few minutes before dividing into two equal pieces.

2. Place one of the pieces of dough in a separate bowl and add the cocoa powder. Combine and knead the cocoa powder into the dough until the whole dough is brown. Cover both bowls with cling film (plastic wrap) and leave to prove for 1 hour, or until slightly increased in size.

3. Take one of your pieces of dough and place on a lightly floured work surface. Roll it out into a rectangle around 25 x 12.5cm (10 x 5in) and 4mm (¼in) thick. Cover it with a damp tea towel to prevent it from drying while you roll out the other piece of dough to the same size and thickness.

4. Place the plain dough on top of the chocolate dough and lightly press to combine the two slightly.

5. Starting at one of the shorter edges, roll the dough up to make a rolled log, then cut the roll into 4 pieces. The spiral should be clear in the centre of the dumpling.

6. Prepare a steamer and line the basket with parchment paper. Place the dumplings into the steamer and steam for 15 minutes.

7. Meanwhile, make the hot chocolate: put the single cream, milk and chopped chocolate into a saucepan and place over a low heat. Stir until the chocolate has melted and combined.

8. When your dumplings are fluffy and cooked, remove from the steamer. Fill your mugs with hot chocolate and top with whipped double cream. Enjoy!

DIETARY SWAPS

VE

V

NV

GF

DF

Chilli Garlic Prawns with Ricotta Puffs (page 46)

Ve	
V	Remove the prawns/shrimp
NV	
GF	Use gluten-free flour and breadcrumbs
DF	

Tofu & Broccoli Dumplings Glazed in Soy & Sesame Seed Dressing (page 48)

Ve	Make sure you use vegan dumpling wrappers
V	
NV	Replace the firm tofu with 100g (3½oz) chicken mince
GF	Use gluten-free dumpling wrappers and soy sauce
DF	

Miso Tofu Soup with Pork & Mushroom Pillows (page 50)

Ve	Replace the pork with tofu or a vegan mince alternative
V	Replace the pork with tofu or a veggie mince alternative
NV	
GF	Use gluten-free wrappers and soy sauce
DF	

Gochujang Sausage Pouches topped with Kimchi (page 53)

Ve	Use vegan sausages and maple syrup instead of honey. Check that the kimchi is vegan
V	Use veggie sausages and check that the kimchi is vegetarian
NV	
GF	Use gluten-free wrappers and soy sauce
DF	

Fiery Leek Pockets with a Spiced Lentil Sauce (page 54)

Ve	Use plant-based yoghurt
V	
NV	Swap the leeks for beef mince (ground beef)
GF	Use my gluten-free wrapper recipe on page 41
DF	Use dairy-free yoghurt

Pork & Water Chestnut 'Dumpling Tacos' (page 56)

Ve	Replace the pork mince (ground pork) with blended firm tofu or a vegan mince alternative and omit the fish sauce
V	Replace the pork mince (ground pork) with blended firm tofu or a vegan mince alternative and omit the fish sauce
NV	
GF	Use gluten-free wrappers and soy sauce
DF	

Crispy Rice Paper Rolls (page 57)

Ve	
V	
NV	Replace the tofu with your choice of minced meat
GF	Use gluten-free soy sauce
DF	

Hoisin Chicken & Chive Crispy Skirt Dumplings (page 58)

Ve	Use a vegan mince alternative and vegan hoisin sauce (or replace with teriyaki or sweet chilli sauce)
V	Use a vegan mince alternative and vegan hoisin sauce (or replace with teriyaki or sweet chilli sauce)
NV	
GF	Use gluten-free wrappers, hoisin sauce and soy sauce
DF	

Teenie Tiny Parcels with Whipped Feta Yoghurt & Paprika Butter (page 61)

Ve	Use a vegan mince alternative and plant-based yoghurt and feta. Omit the butter
V	Use a vegan mince alternative
NV	
GF	Use gluten-free wrappers
DF	Use dairy-free yoghurt and feta

Lemongrass, Beef & Basil 'Cheat' Pan-Fried Buns (page 62)

Ve	Replace the beef mince (ground beef) with a combination of crumbled tofu, finely chopped aubergine (eggplant) and finely chopped mushroom OR a plant-based meat alternative. Use vegan Greek yoghurt like unsweetened soy yoghurt.
V	Replace the beef mince with crumbled tofu or a plant-based meat alternative
NV	
GF	Use gluten-free self-raising (self-rising) flour and soy sauce
DF	Use dairy-free yoghurt

Leek & Aubergine Moon Pouches (page 64)

Ve	
V	
NV	Add some minced pork to the filling
GF	Use gluten-free wrappers and soy sauce
DF	

Dough Clusters in a Creamy Kimchi Bacon & Broccoli Stew (page 65)

Ve	Replace the egg with 80ml (3fl oz) olive oil and the milk with a plant-based alternative. Check that the kimchi is vegan. Swap the bacon for crumbled tofu and smoked paprika. Use a plant-based cream and vegan Parmesan
V	Check that the kimchi is veggie-friendly. Swap the bacon for crumbled tofu and smoked paprika. Use veggie-friendly Parmesan
NV	
GF	Use gluten-free flour
DF	Use dairy-free cream and vegan Parmesan

Open-Ended Chipotle Pork & Aubergine Parcels (page 65)

Ve	Use a vegan mince alternative
V	Use a vegan mince alternative
NV	
GF	Use gluten-free wrappers
DF	

Three-Ingredient Dumplings in a Three-Ingredient Sauce (page 69)

Ve	Use plant-based single (light) cream and a vegan Cheddar alternative
V	
NV	
GF	
DF	Use dairy-free single (light) cream and a vegan Cheddar alternative

Chorizo Butter Bean Dumplings with Tomatoes, Anchovies, and Olives (page 71)

Ve	Replace the chorizo with crumbled tofu and 1 tsp paprika. Make sure your dumpling wrappers are vegan. Omit the anchovies (season with a bit more salt) and use a vegan feta alternative
V	Replace the chorizo with crumbled tofu and 1 tsp paprika. Omit the anchovies (season with a bit more salt)
NV	
GF	Use gluten-free wrappers
DF	Omit the feta or use a dairy-free alternative

Air Fryer Crab Rangoon (page 72)

Ve	
V	
NV	
GF	
DF	Use vegan cream cheese

Twist on a Reuben (page 73)

Ve	
V	Omit the salt beef and use a veggie-friendly Worcestershire sauce
NV	
GF	
DF	

One Pot Spicy Beef Stew with Chilean-Style Dumplings (page 74)

Ve	Replace the beef with finely chopped mushrooms and the beef stock with veggie stock. Use a total of 75ml (3fl oz) water to combine with the flour to make the dough
V	Replace the beef with finely chopped mushrooms and use veggie stock
NV	
GF	Use my gluten-free wrapper recipe on page 41
DF	Omit the sour cream or use a plant-based version

Miso Ragu & Scissor Cut Dumplings (page 77)

Ve	Use minced mushrooms and crumbled tofu instead of beef. Use veggie stock instead of beef stock. Omit the parmesan and/or replace with a vegan alternative
V	Use minced mushrooms and crumbled tofu instead of beef. Use veggie stock instead of beef stock. Omit the parmesan and/or replace with a veggie alternative
NV	
GF	Use my gluten-free wrapper recipe on page 41 and ensure all sauces are gluten-free
DF	Swap the Parmesan for a dairy-free or vegan version

Creamy 'Vori Vori' Cornflour Dumpling Bowl (page 78)

Ve	
V	Replace the chicken breast with portobello mushrooms and use veggie stock instead of chicken. Use veggie-friendly Parmesan
NV	
GF	Make sure the chicken stock is gluten-free
DF	

Cauliflower & Mushroom Dough Balls with a Tomato & Walnut Ragu (page 79)

Ve	Omit the gouda or replace with your favourite vegan cheese. Omit the egg and replace with 40ml (1½fl oz) olive oil. Use plant-based milk
V	
NV	
GF	Use your favourite gluten-free bread to bind the mixture and use my gluten-free wrapper recipe on page 41
DF	Replace the Gouda with your favourite dairy-free cheese

Pea and Ricotta Squares with Crispy Prosciutto (page 80)

Ve	Ensure your dumpling wrappers are vegan. Use a plant-based ricotta. Omit the Parmesan or use a vegan alternative. Use vegan butter and vegan butter for the topping. Omit the prosciutto or use a vegan alternative
V	Use vegan bacon
NV	
GF	Use gluten-free wrappers
DF	Use plant-based ricotta, Parmesan and butter

Buffalo Chicken Triangles with a Blue Cheese Sauce (page 82)

Ve	
V	Replace the chicken mince (ground chicken) with ground fried tofu and mushroom
NV	
GF	Use gluten-free wrappers and check any sauces for gluten
DF	

Rice Noodles, Crispy Air Fryer Dumplings, and a Green Dressing (page 85)

Ve	Use a vegan mince alternative and vegan oyster sauce (or replace with light soy sauce)
V	Use a vegan mince alternative and vegan oyster sauce (or replace with light soy sauce)
NV	
GF	Use gluten-free wrappers and check any sauces for gluten
DF	

Peri Peri Chicken Boats with Burrata (page 86)

Ve	Replace the chicken with crumbled tofu blended with finely chopped mushrooms. Make sure the wrappers are vegan and use vegan burrata
V	Replace the chicken with crumbled tofu blended with finely chopped mushrooms
NV	
GF	Use my gluten-free wrapper recipe on page 41
DF	Omit the burrata or use a dairy-free alternative

Greek Beans Topped with Parmesan Dumplings (page 90)

Ve	
V	
NV	When frying the onion, carrot, leek and garlic, add in 4 roughly chopped herby sausages
GF	
DF	

Crispy Bean Fritters with Sweet Chilli Cavolo Nero & Chickpea Stew (page 93)

Ve	Use vegan Cheddar
V	
NV	Add some cooked chicken to the stew
GF	
DF	Use a plant-based Cheddar alternative

Cumin Pork Dumplings with Homemade Chilli Dip (page 94)

Ve	Use a vegan mince alternative or finely chopped mushrooms and tofu
V	Use a vegan mince alternative or finely chopped mushrooms and tofu
NV	
GF	Use gluten-free wrappers and soy sauce
DF	

Chipotle Chicken & Corn Ball Casserole (page 97)

Ve	Replace the chicken with sliced portobello mushrooms. Use veggie stock, plant-based butter, vegan sour cream and vegan milk
V	Replace the chicken with portobello mushrooms and use veggie stock
NV	
GF	
DF	Replace the sour cream, cream and milk with plant-based alternatives

Layered Lamb Dumpling Bake with a Paprika Tomato Drizzle (page 98)

Ve	Swap out the lamb with a combination of blended mushrooms, tofu, and aubergine (eggplant). Use vegan sour cream, vegan single cream, vegan parmesan (or nutritional yeast) and vegan mozzarella. And lastly, use plant-based butter or olive oil for the paprika butter
V	Swap out the lamb with a combination of blended mushrooms, tofu, and aubergine (eggplant). Use veggie-friendly parmesan
NV	
GF	Use my gluten-free wrapper recipe on page 41
DF	Use dairy-free sour cream, single (light) cream, Parmesan and mozzarella

Toasted Lamb Hats in Yoghurt Sauce Topped with Fennel, Orange & Harissa Dressing (page 100)

Ve	Use a vegan mince alternative and replace with yoghurt with a plant-based yoghurt
V	Use a vegan mince alternative
NV	
GF	Use gluten-free flour and soy sauce (check any other sauces for gluten)
DF	Use a plant-based yoghurt

Pan-Fried Harissa Turkey Dumplings (page 103)

Ve	Use a vegan mince alternative and vegan yoghurt
V	Use a vegan mince alternative
NV	
GF	Use my gluten-free wrapper recipe on page 41
DF	Use dairy-free yoghurt

Pulled Aubergine Steamed Bun (page 106)

Ve	
V	
NV	Add some pork mince (ground pork) to the filling
GF	
DF	

Chicken & Chorizo Bakes with a Chilli Lime Aioli (page 108)

Ve	
V	Replace the chicken and chorizo with your choice of vegetables, plus 1 tsp smoked paprika
NV	
GF	Use store-bought gluten-free puff or shortcrust pastry
DF	

Potato & Ricotta Pockets with Chorizo, Creme Fraiche & Dill (page 111)

Ve	Use plant-based ricotta, sour cream and butter. Replace the chorizo with a vegan alternative or fry crumbled tofu with some smoked paprika. Replace the egg in the dough with 20ml (4 tsp) more water
V	Replace the chorizo with a vegan alternative or fry crumbled tofu with some smoked paprika
NV	
GF	Use my gluten-free wrapper recipe on page 41
DF	Use plant-based ricotta, sour cream and butter

Dumpling Wreath (page 114)

Ve	Replace the beef mince (ground beef) with finely chopped mushrooms and walnuts. Use plant-based yoghurt
V	Replace the beef mince (ground beef) with finely chopped mushrooms and walnuts
NV	
GF	Use my gluten-free wrapper recipe on page 41
DF	Use a dairy-free yoghurt

Gochujang 'Potato-Pillow' Lasagne (page 116)

Ve	Replace the beef mince (ground beef) with finely chopped mushrooms and walnuts. Replace the egg yolk with 2–3 tbsp olive oil. Use plant-based milk, Cheddar and Parmesan. Use plant-based butter and mozzarella cheese too
V	Replace the beef mince (ground beef) with finely chopped mushrooms and walnuts
NV	
GF	Use gluten-free flour and stock
DF	Use plant-based milk and cheese

Open-Top Tofu & Mushroom Baskets with Tahini Chilli Noodles (page 119)

Ve	
V	
NV	
GF	Use gluten-free wrappers and noodles and ensure all other ingredients are gluten-free
DF	

Feta, Mint & Spinach Baked Pockets (page 120)

Ve	Use plant-based feta cheese, parmesan and filo pastry. Omit the eggs and replace with 30ml (2 tbsp) olive oil. Use plant-based butter and replace the honey for agave
V	
NV	
GF	Use gluten-free filo pastry, if you can find it
DF	Use a plant-based feta, parmesan and replace the butter for brushing with oil

Chicken & Lemongrass Pockets in a Fiery Fish Noodle Soup (page 123)

Ve	Instead of chicken mince (ground chicken), either use a plant-based mince alternative, or use blended tofu and mushrooms. Remove the fish sauce or use vegan fish sauce. Ensure the square wrappers are vegan. Replace fish stock with veggie stock
V	Instead of chicken mince (ground chicken), either use a plant-based mince alternative, or use blended tofu and mushrooms. Remove the fish sauce or use vegan fish sauce. Ensure the square wrappers are vegan. Replace fish stock with veggie stock
NV	
GF	Use gluten-free wrappers and ensure the noodles, fish stock and soy sauce are all gluten-free
DF	

Stuffed Potato Boulders with Stir-Fried Sausage Apple & Cabbage (page 124)

Ve	Replace the mozzarella with a plant-based version (or omit it). Use vegan sausages or crumbled tofu in the stir fry
V	Use vegan sausages or crumbled tofu in the stir fry
NV	
GF	Use gluten-free flour
DF	Use a dairy-free mozzarella

Egg Envelopes with a Ginger Pork Filling (page 127)

Ve	
V	Replace the pork mince (ground pork) with a plant-based alternative and use veggie stock
NV	
GF	
DF	

French Onion Dumpling Soup (page 129)

Ve	Replace the butter with more oil, use veggie stock and replace the eggs with around 30ml (2 tbsp) water and 30ml (2 tbsp) olive oil. Use plant-based milk and a vegan Gruyere alternative
V	Replace the beef stock with veggie stock
NV	
GF	
DF	Use plant-based butter, milk and cheese

Mini Jerk Chicken Fried Dumpling Burgers (page 130)

Ve	Use portobello mushrooms instead of chicken and use vegan cheese. Use a vegan alternative to Worcestershire sauce and a vegan mayonnaise
V	Use portobello mushrooms instead of chicken. Use a vegan alternative to Worcestershire sauce
NV	
GF	
DF	Use a dairy-free cheese alternative

Spinach & Artichoke Balls in a butter cream & sage sauce (page 133)

Ve	Use plant based milk and replace the eggs with an additional 50ml (scant 2fl oz) plant-based milk, vegan parmesan, plant-based single (light) cream and butter
V	
NV	
GF	Use gluten-free bread
DF	Use plant-based alternatives for the milk, cheese, cream and butter

Pork & Vermicelli Cabbage Rolls (page 135)

Ve	Replace the pork mince (ground pork) with crumbled tofu. Remove fish sauce or use a vegan alternative
V	Replace the pork mince (ground pork) with crumbled tofu. Remove fish sauce or use a vegan alternative
NV	
GF	Check any sauces for gluten
DF	

Sesame Crisp Squash & Turkey Dumplings in Ginger Broth (page 136)

Ve	Omit the turkey mince (groung turkey) and double up the butternut squash quantities. Replace honey for agave
V	Omit the turkey mince (groung turkey) and double up the butternut squash quantities
NV	
GF	Use gluten-free wrappers and ensure any sauces and stock are gluten-free
DF	

Brothy Spinach & Beef Parcels (page 138)

Ve	Replace the eggs with 100ml (3½fl oz) water. Replace the beef mince (ground beef) with a plant-based alternative, or a mixture of blended walnuts, mushrooms and firm tofu weighing a total of 200g (7oz). Replace the cream cheese with a vegan option. Use veggie stock instead of beef stock. Choose a plant-based sour cream
V	Replace the beef mince (ground beef) with a plant-based alternative, or a mixture of blended walnuts, mushrooms, and firm tofu weighing a total of 200g (7oz). Use veggie stock instead of beef stock
NV	
GF	Use my gluten-free wrapper recipe on page 41
DF	Replace the cream cheese and sour cream with non-dairy alternatives

Blended Chilli Tomato topped with Juicy Chicken Dumplings (page 141)

Ve	Replace the chicken mince (ground chicken) with a blended mixture of carrot, cabbage, and tofu weighing 200g (7oz)
V	Replace the chicken mince (ground chicken) with a blended mixture of carrot, cabbage, and tofu weighing 200g (7oz)
NV	
GF	Use my gluten-free wrapper recipe on page 41 and ensure any sauces are gluten-free
DF	

Paneer & Potato Dumplings in a Cashew Chickpea Tomato Cream (page 142)

Ve	Use a vegan paneer or mozzarella alternative. Use veggie stock and plant-based cream
V	
NV	Adding fried diced chicken to the sauce would be delicious
GF	
DF	Use dairy-free paneer and cream

Chilli Chicken & Sweet Potato Peanut Stew with Fluffy Balls (page 144)

Ve	Replace the chicken thighs with portobello mushrooms, aubergine (eggplant) slices, or torn tofu
V	Replace the chicken thighs with portobello mushrooms, aubergine (eggplant) slices, or torn tofu
NV	
GF	
DF	

'Nduja & Cream Cheese Stuffed Squares with a Cherry Tomato Sauce (page 146)

Ve	Replace the egg with 70ml (2½fl oz) water. Use vduja paste instead of 'nduja and replace the ricotta and Parmesan with vegan alternatives
V	Use vduja paste instead of 'nduja and use a vegetarian Parmesan
NV	
GF	Use my gluten-free wrapper recipe on page 41
DF	Use dairy-free alternatives for the ricotta and Parmesan

Chickpea & Sautéed Onion Dumplings with a Ginger Carrot Sauce (page 149)

Ve	Replace the egg in the dough with 2 tbsp water. Replace the honey with agave or maple syrup and use a plant-based cream
V	
NV	
GF	Use my gluten-free wrapper recipe on page 41 and gluten-free soy sauce
DF	Use a dairy-free cream

Deep-Fried Beef & Parsley Nibbles (page 150)

Ve	
V	
NV	
GF	
DF	Use plant-based butter

The 'Oooof' Dumpling Soup (page 151)

Ve	
V	
NV	
GF	Use my gluten-free wrapper recipe on page 41 and incorporate the ginger, garlic and spring onion (scallion) into it
DF	

Vibrant Dumpling Chaat (page 154)

Ve	Use vegan tortellini and plant-based yoghurt
V	Use vegetarian tortellini
NV	Use meat-filled tortellini
GF	Use gluten-free tortellini
DF	Use dairy-free tortellini and plant-based yoghurt

Zingy Tomato & Crispy Dumpling Salad (page 156)

Ve	Omit the fish sauce and use vegan dumplings
V	Omit the fish sauce and use vegetarian dumplings
NV	
GF	Use gluten-free dumplings
DF	

Steamed Dumplings in a Spicy Tomato Sauce (page 157)

Ve	Use vegan dumplings
V	Use vegetarian dumplings
NV	Use meat-filled dumplings
GF	Use gluten-free dumplings and soy sauce
DF	

No-Fuss Chicken & Dumpling Soup (page 159)

Ve	Replace the chicken breast with firm tofu or oyster mushrooms, the chicken stock with veggie stock and the cream of chicken soup with a vegan cream of mushroom soup
V	Replace the chicken breast with firm tofu or oyster mushrooms, the chicken stock with veggie stock and the cream of chicken soup with a vegan cream of mushroom soup
NV	
GF	Use gluten-free flour and gnocchi
DF	Use dairy-free butter and a vegan cream of mushroom soup

Air Fryer Crunchy Dumplings with Green Tahini (page 160)

Ve	Use vegan dumplings
V	Use vegetarian dumplings
NV	Use meat-filled dumplings
GF	Use gluten-free-dumplings
DF	

Easy Hot & Sour Soup Dumplings (page 163)

Ve	Use vegan dumplings and omit the eggs
V	Use vegetarian dumplings
NV	
GF	Use gluten-free dumplings and gluten-free soy sauce
DF	

Speedy Harissa Aubergine, Butter Bean & Dumpling Stew (page 164)

Ve	Use vegan dumplings
V	Use vegetarian dumplings
NV	Use meat-filled dumplings
GF	Use gluten-free dumplings
DF	

Crispy Korean-Style Dumpling & Soba Noodle Salad (page 167)

Ve	Use vegan dumplings
V	Use vegetarian dumplings
NV	Use meat-filled dumplings
GF	Use gluten-free dumplings and soy sauce
DF	

Chipotle Feta Courgettes with Cannellini Beans & Dumplings (page 168)

Ve	Use vegan dumplings and plant-based feta
V	
NV	Use meat-filled dumplings
GF	Use gluten-free dumplings
DF	Use dairy-free feta

Homemade Chilli Hummus with Crispy Lamb & Dumplings (page 171)

Ve	Replace the lamb mince (ground lamb) with crumbled tofu and use vegan dumplings
V	Replace the lamb mince (ground lamb) with crumbled tofu and use vegan dumplings
NV	
GF	Use gluten-free dumplings
DF	

Shiitake Alfredo Dumplings (page 172)

Ve	Use vegan dumplings and plant-based butter, cream and Parmesan
V	Use vegetarian dumplings and vegetarian Parmesan
NV	
GF	Use gluten-free dumplings
DF	Use dairy-free butter, cream and Parmesan

Dumpling Caesar Salad (page 173)

Ve	Use vegan dumplings and tempeh instead of bacon. Use vegan mayo, vegan cream cheese instead of cottage cheese, vegan Parmesan and omit the anchovy (season with a little more salt)
V	Use vegetarian dumplings, tempeh instead of bacon and vegetarian Parmesan. Omit the anchovy (season with a little more salt)
NV	
GF	Use gluten-free dumplings
DF	Use dairy-free cream cheese instead of cottage cheese and vegan Parmesan

Sweet 'Nduja Dumplings with Aubergine & Yoghurt (page 174)

Ve	Use vegan dumplings and vduja instead of 'nduja, maple syrup instead of honey and a plant-based thick yoghurt
V	Use vegetarian dumplings and vduja instead of 'nduja
NV	
GF	Use gluten-free dumplings
DF	Use dairy-free yoghurt

Salsa Verde Dumplings (page 177)

Ve	Use vegan dumplings and omit the eggs. Use plant-based feta
V	Use vegetarian dumplings
NV	
GF	Use gluten-free dumplings
DF	Use dairy-free feta

Speedy Laksa-Style Dumpling Noodle Soup (page 178)

Ve	Use vegan Thai curry paste, veggie stock and omit the fish sauce and egg. Use vegan dumplings and oyster mushrooms instead of the prawns (shrimp)
V	Use vegan Thai curry paste, veggie stock and omit the fish sauce and egg. Use vegan dumplings and oyster mushrooms instead of the prawns (shrimp)
NV	
GF	Use gluten-free dumplings
DF	

Surprise Apricot Bombs (page 183)

Ve	Use vegan butter and cream cheese. Replace the egg in the dumpling dough with 30ml water. Serve with vegan custard
V	
NV	
GF	
DF	Replace the cream cheese, butter and custard with dairy-free alternatives

Maple Syrup & Bacon Bake (page 184)

Ve	Replace the butter, milk and ice cream with plant-based alternatives. For the bacon, either use a vegan substitute from the supermarket, or fry some finely crumbled tofu in a pan with smoked paprika and ½ tsp sugar
V	For the bacon, either use a vegan substitute from the supermarket, or fry some finely crumbled tofu in a pan with smoked paprika and ½ tsp sugar
NV	
GF	
DF	Use dairy-free butter, milk and ice cream

Mini Biscoff Fried Dumplings (page 187)

Ve	Omit the egg and replace with 30ml (2 tbsp) water. Use vegan butter and plant-based milk
V	
NV	
GF	
DF	Replace the butter and milk with plant-based alternatives

Ginger Ale Baked Apple & Blackberry Dumplings (page 188)

Ve	Use a store-bought vegan shortcrust or puff pastry and use that as the dough. Use plant-based ice cream or custard to serve
V	
NV	
GF	Use a gluten-free store-bought shortcrust or puff pastry dough
DF	Use plant-based butter and milk in the dough and dairy-free ice cream or custard

Cottage Cheese, Almond & Orange Dumplings (page 189)

Ve	
V	
NV	
GF	
DF	

Tiramisu-Style Rice Flour Pillows (page 190)

Ve	Use vegan alternatives for the mascarpone, cream, sponge fingers and milk
V	
NV	
GF	Use gluten-free sponge fingers
DF	Use dairy-free alternatives for the mascarpone, cream and milk

Blueberry & Raisin Parcels with Sour Cream & Flaked Almonds (page 193)

Ve	Omit the egg from the dough and increase the water to 100ml (3½fl oz). Replace the butter and sour cream with vegan alternatives
V	
NV	
GF	Use my gluten-free wrapper recipe on page 41
DF	Replace the butter and sour cream with dairy-free alternatives

Cardamom & Orange Syrup Dumplings (page 194)

Ve	
V	
NV	
GF	
DF	

Nostalgic Lemon Dumplings (page 197)

Ve	Use vegan Greek yoghurt, double (heavy) cream and lemon curd
V	
NV	
GF	
DF	Use plant-based yoghurt, cream and lemon curd

Chocolate Spiral Buns (page 199)

Ve	Replace the milk, cream and chocolate with vegan alternatives
V	
NV	
GF	
DF	Replace the milk, cream and chocolate with dairy-free alternatives

INDEX

ACKNOWLEDGEMENTS

I would never have been able to do this alone. Yes, my name is on the front of this book, but let's be honest, it should have been a whole list of people that have put their heart and soul into *The World Is Your Dumpling*. So, let's begin with the thank yous!

To Emily Sweet, my literary agent (and Amelia who introduced us!!), for always having my back, being a brilliant cheerleader, and taking a chance on working with me to try something new. A huge thank you to Lydia Good, my publisher at HarperCollins, who saw the vision for this book from day dot and has made it what it is today.

To Liz and Max Haarala Hamilton who made the dumplings come to life and filled the shoot with laughs, giggles, and unlimited positivity. Your studio now feels like a second home. To Hanna Miller (aka expedition leader), for your strategic prepping, measuring and re-measuring, for trekking all over London to pick out all the ingredients, and for making these little parcels of joy look so moorish and delightful to eat. Thank you to Eden, Val, and Alice for your joyful and wonderful food styling assistance. To Jennifer Kay who plucked out the best props that made the dumplings pop!

Sim Greenaway, the creative genius who turned colours, words, and images into the most gorgeous, fun, and vibrant book design. Thank you to Sarah Hammond (dump-pea) and the proof-reader team for transforming my melting pot of words into an actual book to be proud of. To Dani Mestriner and Hetty Touquet, queens of publicity and marketing who helped spread the dumpling word out to the world! Thank you to everyone else at HarperCollins and beyond who have turned this book into what it is today ... you're all the best!!

Thank you to Noya, for being a role model and absolute boss in the kitchen. My time at Noya's Kitchen was unforgettable and you taught me so much about the world of food and hospitality. I miss seeing your smiley face and can't wait for you to do a book!

The foodie community. Where do I begin? You guys have been instrumental in making this job an absolute dream. The support, love, laughter, and care I receive from each and every one of you is beyond incredible. So thank you!! But I have to mention one gal in particular: Mimi Harrison, who not only came up with the beautiful title 'The World Is Your Dumpling' but has been there for me endlessly throughout the stress and excitement of this book. You're an angel and I adore you.

Thank you to my fabulous cheerleading squad, aka my best friends: Zoe, Tiana, Leonie, and Tats, you've all been such positive queens and showered me with compliments, supportive messages, and celebratory gifts throughout the entire book journey. I'm the luckiest girl to have such thoughtful and gorgeous friends. I'm so sorry I don't have the page count to name all of my other beautiful friends, but IYKYK!! Thank you besties!

I am so unbelievably lucky to have the best and most supportive family. Carole & Christopher aka Muma and Papa, you have both been the most inspirational and positive parents I could ever ask for. Your work ethic encourages me to do better every day. Nic Nacs, the number one sister in the world, with unlimited smiles and motivation whenever I've felt overwhelmed. From the celebratory cakes to the homemade cards, you're a star in and out. To Granny, Susanne, Anthony, and Rollie for always believing in me, I hope I've made you proud. Thank you to Charlie and Morgan for being fabulous recipe testers, you've both shown so much love

and I really really appreciate you so much for that. To the rest of my incredible wider family, all the cousins, you guys are THE BEST and I'm so fortunate to have such a supportive cluster of people around me. To the best god mothers a girl could ask for, Alison and Annalisa, you have been pillars of inspiration throughout my life and I really hope you appreciate how big of a part you've played in motivating me to set goals and be the best person I can be.

Thank you to Matt, Jo, Immie, Digby, Alfie, and Arthur for your endless support. Jo, you're my number one Instagram fan with your lovely comments and supportive messages. I hugely appreciate them, lots of love!

To Henry, my chief recipe tester, my partner, my love. You have been my hype man on the good days and my rock on the slightly more stressful 'omg I'm going to have a breakdown' days. Thank you for being by my side for every step of the way, your support has been unconditional and I am so grateful. I love you.

Last but absolutely not least, to everyone from my online community, who kept cooking, sharing, liking, following, and subscribing: thank you for turning my dream into a reality and supporting me on this journey. Literally, none of this would have happened without you and I owe you all so many hugs. With love and dumplings, Em xx

HarperCollins*Publishers*
1 London Bridge Street
London SE1 9GF

www.harpercollins.co.uk

HarperCollins*Publishers*
Macken House, 39/40 Mayor Street
Upper, Dublin 1, D01 C9W8, Ireland

First published by HarperCollins*Publishers*
2024

10 9 8 7 6 5 4 3 2 1

Text © Emily Roz 2024
Photography © Haarala Hamilton 2024

Emily Roz asserts the moral right to be
identified as the author of this work

A catalogue record of this book is
available from the British Library

ISBN 978-0-00-870014-0

Food Stylist: Hanna Miller
Prop Stylist: Jennifer Kay
Illustrations: Shutterstock.com

Printed and bound by GPS
in Bosnia & Herzegovina

This book is produced from
independently certified FSC™ paper to
ensure responsible forest management.

For more information visit: www.
harpercollins.co.uk/green

WHEN USING KITCHEN APPLIANCES
PLEASE ALWAYS FOLLOW THE
MANUFACTURER'S INSTRUCTIONS